THE FINITUDE OF BEING

**SUNY Series in
Contemporary Continental Philosophy**

Dennis J. Schmidt, Editor

THE FINITUDE OF BEING

JOAN STAMBAUGH

STATE UNIVERSITY OF NEW YORK PRESS

Production by Ruth Fisher
Marketing by Dana E. Yanulavich

Acknowledgment: The epilogue, originally conceived as part of this study, was published by The Eastern Buddhist, Kyoto, Japan. Permission is gratefully acknowledged.

Published by
State University of New York Press, Albany

For information, address the State University of New York Press,
State University Plaza, Albany, NY 12246

Library of Congress Cataloging-in-Publication Data
Stambaugh, Joan, 1932–
    The finitude of being / Joan Stambaugh.
        p.   cm. — (SUNY series in contemporary continental
philosophy)
    Includes bibliographical references and index.
    ISBN 0-7914-1105-2 (hard : alk. paper). — ISBN 0-7914-1106-0
(pbk. : alk. paper)
    1. Heidegger, Martin, 1889–1976—Contributions in concept of the
finite.   2. Finite, The—History—20th century.   I. Title.
II. Series.
B3279.H49S634   1992
111'.6'092—dc20   91-26008
                                                              CIP

10 9 8 7 6 5 4 3 2 1

Henry Rosenthal

in memoriam

and for

Ria Stavrides

CONTENTS

The Problem   1

Throughout a lifetime of writings, despite other fairly radical
changes of perspective, Heidegger has always consistently maintained that being is finite. To say that something is finite generally
means that it is limited. Although this is consonant with what
Heidegger means, it by no means exhausts or even gets close to his
view. Given his conception of time and space, a conception that is
quite different from traditional views, finitude cannot mean only
that something objectively present has limits in space and time. To
begin with, being is in no possible sense of the word a being or a
thing. Thus, these two points—the radically altered conception of
time and space, and the fact that being cannot be represented as an
objectively present being or thing—make it necessary to inquire
into a meaning of finitude that goes beyond mere limitation in time
and space.

   Heidegger first became known in this country through the
theologians who thought that being might be equivalent to God. For
example, the Protestant theologian Paul Tillich said that the only
nonsymbolic statement that could be made about God was that God
was being. Heidegger, for his part, once said somewhere: How can
we talk about God when we don't even know what being is? Apart
from this, Heidegger stated in *Being and Time:*

> We do not need to discuss in detail the fact that the traditional
> concept of eternity in the significance of the 'standing now'
> (*nunc stans*) is drawn from the vulgar understanding of time
> and defined in orientation toward the idea of 'constant' objec-
> tive presence. If the eternity of *God* could be philosophically
> 'constructed,' it could be understood only as primordial and 'in-
> finite' temporality. Whether or not the *via negationis et emi-
> nentiae* could offer a possible way remains an open question.[1]

However, Heidegger never pursued the question of primordial
and infinite temporality, but adhered stringently to the finitude of
being for the rest of his philosophical life.

If the finitude of being does not lie in its being limited in time and space as they have been traditionally conceived, we might more properly look for it in the dimension of truth. Truth, for Heidegger, does not mean the traditional correspondence theory of truth where something is true if the idea that I have in my head corresponds to an object in the outside world. This correspondence theory of truth states that truth is having a correct idea of an object that corresponds to the actual object. For Heidegger, truth consists in the fact that things are disclosed to us at all in the first place. Thus, truth is something very much akin to revelation, or, to use a more neutral and less biblical term, to unconcealment. But things are never simply unconcealed or disclosed to us; they are at the same time concealed, hidden from us. This is generally Heidegger's view, and it may point to some sort of duality in his conception of being. This duality may be the condition of all disclosure: There can be no disclosure or unconcealment without simultaneous concealment. If this is so—and it probably is—then we need to inquire further into the implications of this.

On the other hand, there is a fundamental term in late Heidegger corresponding to disclosure and unconcealment that does not appear to have a counterconcept. That term is 'Lichtung', 'clearing' or 'opening.' In the course of conversations with Heidegger about translation problems, it became increasingly evident that he was very excited about this word, which indicated, to me at least, that he had discovered something new that went beyond his general concept of unconcealment. It is not a question of 'development' here, from unconcealment to *Lichtung;* both terms are used concurrently.

However, the overwhelming evidence is clearly on the side of concealment as lying at the heart of being. Any attempt at developing the implications of *Lichtung* conceived as free of concealment, which will be explored later in this study, goes beyond what Heidegger actually said and, as such, must remain purely speculative.

In the lecture course *The Basic Concepts of Metaphysics*, given in 1929–30, Heidegger discusses three concepts: world, finitude, and solitude or individuality. Fascinating as these lectures are (especially the sections on animals), they do not tell us very much about finitude. Finitude is thought primarily with regard to human being, not with regard to being itself. In fact, there is little emphasis on being itself in these lectures, which may well be the reason why Eugen Fink regarded them so highly, repeatedly urging Heidegger to publish them.

Although it is one of the three concepts constituting the title of these lectures, finitude is not developed in them to any significant degree. We are told that it is the root of the other two, world and solitude or individuality, and that it consists fundamentally in the brokenness (*Gebrochenheit*) of *Dasein*. By the brokenness of *Dasein* Heidegger means that the expanse of *Dasein's* horizon is broken by the moment which brings it to authentic existence. Here we see that it is precisely its finitude that enables *Dasein* to attain authentic existence. Finitude is never simply a limited, 'negative' characteristic for Heidegger, especially since the 'positive' counterpart, infinity, is totally absent from his thought.

The most significant statement about finitude in these lectures occurs in the context of a critique of Kant and Hegel—more specifically, a critique of a presumed infinity obtained through the use of dialectic. We should recall that already in *Being and Time*, Heidegger had called dialectic "the embarrassment of philosophy."

Hegel's step from Kant to absolute idealism is the sole consistency of the development of Western philosophy. This development is *possible* and *necessary* through Kant because the problem of human *Dasein*, finitude, did not become a real problem for him and thus not a central problem of philosophy because Kant himself—as the second edition of the *Critique of Pure Reason* shows—encouraged the path of working his way out of an uncomprehended finitude to appeasing himself with infinity. . . . This consistency is necessary and admirable in the way Hegel develops it, yet as consistency it is already the sign of a presumed infinity. In-consistency belongs to finitude, not as a lack or an embarrassment but as an active force. Finitude makes dialectic impossible, shows it to be illusion. In-consequence, lack of ground and fundamental concealment belong to finitude.[2]

Kant did not take finitude seriously as an ultimate characteristic of human being not to be overcome. Hegel dispensed with it altogether. The step from critical to absolute idealism simply threw out the thing-in-itself and let it appear as the development of Absolute Spirit. In rejecting this step, Heidegger names three characteristics of finitude which will play a major role in his later thought: in-consequence, lack of ground, and fundamental concealment. We have here a first indication that finitude fundamentally has to do with concealment.

In-consequence (*In-konsequenz*, or *Un-folge*), which is less specifically developed in Heidegger's later thought than lack of ground and fundamental concealment, points to the fact that the manner of occurrence of finitude cannot be neatly fitted into anything like the dialectical scheme of 'in itself', 'for itself', 'in and for itself'. This scheme permits the derivation and calculation of each step from its predecessor. Such a calculating prediction is incommensurable with the nature of finitude.

'Lack of ground' (*Grundlosigkeit*) is a more precise and at the same time more comprehensive formulation of what Heidegger was getting at with the term 'in-consequence'. Philosophy should stop trying to give reasons why for everything, in the sense of explaining everything in terms of the objective presence of a connection of cause and effect. The fullest discussion of this question can be found in the lecture course *Der Satz vom Grund*. The movement is to be away from explanation, in the direction of clarification and Heidegger's own unique brand of hermeneutical interpretation: emplacement (*Erörterung*). Lack of ground is epitomized in Angelus Silesius's poem:

> The rose is without a why;
> it blooms because it blooms.

The rose has no why; it just blooms since that is what roses 'do'.

The lecture course that really grapples with the question of finitude as concealment is the one on Parmenides. There we discover that concealment itself is profoundly ambiguous. It has a positive and a negative function; Heidegger does not explicitly distinguish them from one another, nor does he even relate them to each other. This might be his intention; on the other hand, it is certainly something that bears looking into. The question becomes, What is the meaning of concealment, what does it mean that there is concealment in being?

Heidegger's own articulation of the question of *aletheia* gives us four directives. We state these four in order to gain clarity as to his particular approach. Then we want to distance ourselves from them, to a certain extent, by adopting a slightly different perspective on the same factors he is analyzing. Heidegger's articulation of the four directives is as follows:

1. un-*concealment*. The emphasis is on concealment which is itself subdivided into:

        a) concealment as covering over
        b) concealment as protecting
2. *un*-concealment. The emphasis is on the *un-*, the negation of concealment which itself is subdivided into:
        a) removal of concealment
        b) keeping concealment at bay, not allowing it to arise
3. *aletheia* as the strife between concealing and unconcealing
4. the Open

We take the division between (*a*) and (*b*) in (1) to be a substantive distinction between distortion and preservation. The shift in emphasis between (1) and (2), the shift between un-*concealment* and *un*-concealment, can be transposed to (3) as the question of the emphasis in strife. Four is the directive that interests me the most and is almost impossible to document authentically: the Open or Opening (clearing) as being itself. Thus, the order that we wish to pursue is as follows:

1. concealing as preservation
2. strife between concealing and unconcealing
3. concealing as distortion

These three different emphases show that there is no single univocal meaning for the term 'finitude' in Heidegger. All that we can be certain of is that he maintained that finitude without exception. The question for this study then becomes, What did finitude ultimately mean, for Heidegger?

Bearing in mind Heidegger's fundamental distaste for questions of value and for value judgments in general—a distaste that expressed itself very early and in no uncertain terms in *Being and Time* with the refusal to deem inauthenticity inferior to, or less desirable than, authenticity—one tends to be hesitant about assessing these different senses of finitude. But, inevitably, the following thoughts might come to mind.

re 1. Concealing as preservation is a desirable and acceptable meaning. Being should not be thought as something that depletes and exhausts itself in giving; it should be thought as having the resources to preserve and renew itself. After all, there is nothing negative expressed in Heidegger's favorite Heraclitus fragment, "Nature loves to hide." The fragment rather expresses the intriguing thought that there is something playful about Nature. Playfulness is nothing negative. It abounds in Hindu thought and can even be richly documented in Heidegger himself.

re 3) Concealing as distortion is a disturbing and disquieting, if not downright ominous, meaning. Two possible explanations for this tendency of distortion come to mind. Based on the habit of theological thinking, one could infer the existence of something like evil in being. Or one might have to draw the conclusion that there is some kind of impotence, some kind of inability to prevent distortion.

re 2) The strife between concealing and unconcealing lends itself less easily to such value judgments. Yet one would eventually have to ask what it means that there is such a duality between concealing and unconcealing in being itself. The theologian Paul Tillich dealt with this problem of duality with regard to being and nonbeing by stating that being without nonbeing would be a lifeless, static reality incapable of revealing itself and by asserting that being itself is ultimately beyond the duality of being and nonbeing and includes them both. But Heidegger is no theologian and his answers do not fit as neatly as Tillich's.

Lastly, we shall embark upon the speculative and questionable enterprise of inquiring into the clearing as being itself. Before that, we shall have to say something about concealing as (1) a process and (2) a structure. This will complete the scope of what this study is trying to do.

Concealment as Preservation

2

We are dealing here with three terms all having the same root: *bergen,* to preserve and shelter; *entbergen,* to unconceal; and *verbergen,* to conceal. Heidegger does not appear to make a sharp distinction between the two terms opposing unconcealing: 'preserving' and 'concealing'. Whereas preserving has a univocally positive, saving function, the situation is not so clear in the case of concealment, which can generate such negative possibilities as distorting, veiling, and covering over, as well as remain the neutral counterpart of unconcealing. The terms 'negative' and 'positive', which Heidegger would most emphatically reject, are used as makeshift designations of a possible divergence in the meaning of concealment. Concealment as preservation is positive in that it is conducive to protecting and saving beings. Concealment is negative in that it perpetrates distortion, error, and confusion. Eventually we shall try to supplant these familiar and comprehensible but inadequate terms with more appropriate ones.

We might begin with a quote that embodies the ambiguity—that of preservation and distortion—inherent in concealment and then go on to investigate the element of preservation first.

> The word 'unconcealing' *(Ent-bergung)* is ambiguous in that it names what is twofold and belongs together: on the one hand as *un*-concealment the negation of a concealing *(lethe)*, the negation first of all of withdrawing concealing *(lethe)*, then also of *dis*placing and *dis*torting concealing *(pseudos)*; on the other hand, however, as un-*concealing,* preserving, i.e., receiving and keeping in unconcealment.[1]

First of all, a boring but unavoidable necessary word about the German term in question here: the root verb is *bergen,* to preserve, keep, shelter, save. *In sich bergen* simply means to contain. The basic meaning is to enclose something and thus shelter, preserve, and save it. This term is unambiguous. *Verborgenheit* is some kind of intensification of *bergen* and means to conceal. This concealing is ambiguous. It can mean either to shelter and protect thoroughly or to conceal to the point of distorting, disfiguring, deceiving. Then there is *Unverborgenheit,* which is unambiguous and means unconcealment. Lastly, we have the verb *entbergen,* which is, again, ambiguous in a very special sense, and means to unconceal. The special ambiguity in unconcealing is not patently oppositional as in the case of sheltering versus distorting. This unconcealing is not simply a releasing and letting emerge into unconcealment, but it is at the same time a sheltering within that unconcealment. Heidegger's example for this has no counterpart in English that I can think of.

> At first this word (*Entbergung*) might and could just say unhiddenness, (*Ent-hehlung*), and removal of hiddenness, i.e., of concealment. But un-concealing does not just mean removing and getting rid of concealment. We must *at the same time* think un-concealing like 'igniting' (*Ent-zünden*) and 'developing' (*Ent-falten*). Igniting is to bring to ignition; developing: to let the folds of the manifold first emerge in its manifoldness. Un-concealing is *on the one hand against concealing,* like clarifying is against confusing. But unconcealing does not simply yield something unconcealed. Rather *Ent*bergen is as the same time Ent*bergen,* like inflaming (*Entflammen*), which does not get rid of flames, but brings flames to their presencing. Unconcealing is at the same time 'for' preserving what is *unconcealed* in the *unconcealment* of *presencing,* i.e., in being. *What is unconcealed first comes to presence as a being in such preserving.* 'Un-concealing'—this means now at the same time *to bring to a shelter:* namely, to *preserve* what is unconcealed in unconcealment.[2]

To put this as clearly as possible:

Unambiguous	Ambiguous
Bergen—preserve, save	*Verborgenheit*—shelter thoroughly distort
Unverborgenheit—unconcealment	*Entbergen*—unconceal preserve in unconcealment

Again, the ambiguity in *Verborgenheit* and *Entbergen* is different: In *Verborgenheit* it is clearly oppositional in the sense of two mutually exclusive possibilities; in *Entbergen* it is more differentiation than opposition and could perhaps be characterized tentatively as a constitutive polarity.

After this brief excursion into the intricacies that Heidegger has exposed us to here, we shall concentrate on preservation. Now that we are aware of the complexity involved and of the impossibility of any neat, simplistic "solutions," we can proceed to try to gain as much clarity as possible.

> But there is a kind of concealing through which what is concealed is by no means removed and annihilated, but preserved and saved in its own being. This concealing does not make us lose the matter like distorting and disfiguring, withdrawing and removing. This concealing preserves. . . .
>
> Perhaps there are *ways of concealing* that not only preserve, store and thus in a certain way withdraw, but rather *let approach and give something essential in a unique way.*[3]

Here Heidegger cautiously indicates a dimension of concealing that protects and preserves. Although this dimension is less emphasized and certainly less developed than its distorting counterpossibility, it is nevertheless present. Unfortunately, Heidegger does not seem to consider explicitly the relation of these two possibilities of concealing.

> We only wanted to show that unconcealment has as its 'opposite' not only concealing in the sense of distorting and falsehood; rather, there are ways of concealing that not only are of a different kind, but also have nothing about them of the specifically 'negative character' of falsehood and distortion.[4]

There are kinds of concealing that have nothing to do with distortion or falsification. Although Heidegger has less to say about this kind of concealing, he intimates that it is the primordial kind of which the other kinds are derivative.

> Only where a humanity is admitted to the essence of having the word, *logon echein,* is it directed to the preservation of the unconcealment of beings. Only where the directing holds sway and unconcealment appears in it as being itself, does

concealing presence in a way that can never be the merely contrary and unruly opposite to unconcealing in the manner of distortion, disfiguration, of false paths, of deception and falsification.[5]

We are told that when beings appear as unconcealment itself, concealing retains a character that is quite different in essence from its more prevalent forms of distortion and deception. The people who experienced this unconcealment as being and concealing as a sheltering factor belonging to that unconcealment were the Greeks. But, according to Heidegger, the Greeks never articulated this kind of concealing. Still, the sheltering function of concealing was once possible and, we may surmise, has not been active since.

Rising as such is already inclined toward self-closing. The former is concealed in the latter. *Kruptesthai* is, as self-concealing, not a mere self-closing but a sheltering in which the essential possibility of rising is preserved—to which rising as such belongs. Self-concealing guarantees self-revealing its true nature. . . . Still, we are thinking *phusis* superficially if we think it as merely rising and letting rise, and if we continue to attribute qualities of any kind to it. By doing that we overlook what is decisive: that fact that self-revealing not only never dispenses with concealing, but actually needs it, in order to occur essentially in the way it occurs as dis-closing.[6]

Phusis is not to be thought as arising and unconcealing alone. Unconcealing not only does not overcome and banish concealing, but it *needs* concealing in order to presence. We are not told exactly *how* unconcealing needs concealing. The relation can not be thought as any kind of causality; it is "poetically" characterized as *phulei* "loving," which Heidegger interprets as favoring, a kind of relation that appears frequently in his writings.

A final quote can instantiate this view of concealing as an essential ingredient preserving the possibility of unconcealing.

Rising neither abandons nor lets setting go, but rising itself submerges in self-concealing as what makes its presencing possible and fastens itself there. . . . Rising incorporates self-concealing because it can rise only from self-concealing. . . . Without the guarantee of closure and its constant presencing, rising would have to cease to be what it is.[7]

In this passage Heidegger is still speaking the Kantian language of what makes possible. The conception permeates *Being and Time* and was only gradually, perhaps reluctantly, relinquished in the later works. It was replaced by a literal reading of *Ermöglichung* (making possible) in terms of *Mögen*, favoring, liking.

To embrace a 'thing' or a 'person' in its essence means to love it, to favor it. Thought in a more original way, such favoring (*Mögen*) means to bestow essence as a gift. Such favoring is the proper essence of enabling, which not only can achieve this or that but also can let something essentially unfold in its provenance, that is, let it be. It is on the 'strength' of such enabling by favoring that something is properly able to be. This enabling is what is properly 'possible' (*das Mögliche*), that whose essence resides in favoring.[8]

Heidegger interprets the possible not in its logically and metaphysically thought contrast to actuality, but rather as being itself presiding over thinking and its relation to being. We shall return to this nonmetaphysical relation later. We turn now to an 'intermediate' conception of concealing. The extent to which these three conceptions of concealing—preservation, distorting, and an intermediate position between the two—can be sharply differentiated is limited.

Finally, there are a few passages where Heidegger goes so far as to say that it is self-concealing that grants *phusis*, clearly giving concealing priority over *phusis* and unconcealing.[9] Heidegger also adds that *phusis* cannot be thought in its root without self-concealing.[10]

Concealing as Strife with Unconcealing   3

Midway between the conceptions of concealment as preserving and as distorting lies by far the most prevalent conception of a fundamental *strife* between concealment and unconcealment. Here, concealment is thought not so much as a factor preserving and granting unconcealment as an opposing force fully equal in status to unconcealing. The main inspiration for this conception seems to be Heraclitus's saying, "Nature loves to hide" (*phusis kruptesthai philei*).

The plurality of possible meanings of concealing and concealment is expressed in a passage from the lecture course on Parmenides, again, without clear differentiation.

> Somehow we are familiar with concealing and concealment. (1) We know it as hiding, veiling, as covering, but also (2) in the forms of preserving, protecting, of holding back, of entrusting and of delivering over. We are familiar with concealing in the many forms of closing off and closure. . . . (3) Then the word 'unconcealment' refers to the fact that something like supersession and removal of concealment belongs to what the Greeks experienced as the essence of truth. . . . 'Unconcealment' can mean that concealment is taken away, removed, overcome, banned, all of these activities being essentially different. (4) 'Unconcealment' can also mean that concealment is not admitted at all, that it, which is possible and constantly threatens, does not exist and cannot arise. From the manifoldness of the significance of the prefix 'Un' we can easily see that Un-concealment is difficult to define in this regard. And yet a fundamental trait of the essence of un-concealment emerges precisely here that we must expressly capture in order to experience the Greek root essence of 'truth.' This opposition presences in un-concealment itself. Some sort of strife with concealment and concealing holds sway in the essence of truth as un-concealment.[1]

Heidegger has stated that in translating the word *aletheia* we were directed toward four factors:

1) hiding, veiling, covering
2) preserving, protecting, holding back, entrusting, delivering over
3) removal of concealment
4) nonadmission of concealment

The first two meanings of concealment correspond roughly to what we have distinguished as distortion and preserving. The third and fourth meanings name an absence of concealment, either by removing it or by not letting it arise at all, by suppressing it. The clearest thing that emerges from these four meanings is the fact that there is some kind of strife between concealing and unconcealing. We shall retain the two meanings of concealment that we have distinguished (distortion and preservation) and then turn to the third meaning that thinks concealing in its unity with unconcealing as strife. Subsequent to this we shall discuss distortion.

But first a more apocalyptic, soteriological dimension of preservation needs to be pointed out, that of 'saving' (retten). The reason for using such dramatic words as 'apocalyptic' and 'soteriological' here is that the implication is one of rescuing what is unconcealed from being enveloped by total concealment and withdrawal. 'Saving' is meant not merely in the sense of not spending (money) or not using and wearing ("I am saving this hat for wear on special occasions") but of rescuing from danger.

> According to the experience of Greek thinkers this thinking always remains a saving of what is unconcealed from concealment in the sense of obscuring withdrawal.[2]

> But because *aletheia* is the overcoming of *lethe,* what is unconcealed must be saved and drawn into unconcealment and be sheltered in it. Man can relate himself to being as what is unconcealed only by constantly thinking toward the unconcealment of what is unconcealed, i.e. *idea and eidos,* thus saving beings from the withdrawal into concealment.[3]

We shall return to this question of rescue, of soteriology, again when we come to discuss concealment as distortion. We are having the same difficulty that besets Heidegger: it is very difficult, if not impossible, to keep these different meanings of concealing distinct from each other. It is also difficult to try to analyze concealing apart from its relation to unconcealing. We have attempted this and turn now to the question of the strife between concealing and unconcealing.

In this section, we shall try to look at the relation between concealing and unconcealing and try not to be concerned with whether concealing implies preserving and saving or distortion. This issue is going to become still more complex later on. We are by no means finished with it.

The emphasis with regard to the strife between concealing and unconcealing is on the equality of their status. One is never to be found without the other. They form a structural duality in the heart of being.

> 'Truth' is never objectively present 'in itself,' of itself, but fought out (*erstritten*). Unconcealment is wrested from conceal-ment in strife with it. Unconcealment is not fought out in the general sense that men search for truth and fight for it. Rather, what is sought and fought for is in itself strife, uncon-cealment in its essence, quite apart from man's battle for it. Who is fighting there and how the fighters fight remains ob-scure. But we want finally to think this conflicting essence of truth that has shone in the stillest of all lights for two thou-sand years. We want explicitly to experience the strife occur-ring in the essence of truth.[4]

The presencing of truth occurs as strife. The basic thought here seems to be that without unconcealment nothing would be re-vealed at all. Without unconcealment, things not only would not be *known;* they would not *be,* in any coherent or even possible sense of that word. And without concealment things would, so to speak, again disappear, this time into boundless unconcealment. Without the limit and 'backward pull' of concealment, there would be no boundaries within which alone things can be, in the Greek sense of what is. We know, and not only from Heidegger, that the Greeks had no positive connotations of the term 'infinity'. To be means to have limits (*peras*).

In a passage listing three of the four directives, it almost be-comes difficult to see what the differences between them are. They all share in the strife between concealing and unconcealing.

> *Firstly,* un-*concealment* refers to concealment. Thus, conceal-ment holds sway in the root essence of truth.

*Secondly, un-*concealment refers to the fact that it is wrested from concealment and in strife with it. The root essence of truth is strifelike. We must question what 'strife' means here.

Thirdly, in accordance with the aforementioned determinations unconcealment refers to a realm of 'opposites' in which 'truth' stands.[5]

Far from being sharply demarcated from each other, these directives all express the oppositional and strifelike character of concealing and unconcealing. Later on in the same text Heidegger can say:

Unconcealing and concealing are a fundamental trait of being.[6]

Beyond the characterization of the relation of concealing and unconcealing as strife, Heidegger does not seem to try to develop that relation further. In accordance with his rejection of dialectic ("the embarrassment of philosophy"), the opposites of concealment and unconcealment cannot have the relation of mediation. There is no possible third factor as a synthesis.

For *a-letheia...*is itself grounded in its essence in *lethe.* Between the two there is no mediation and no transition, because both belong to each other immediately in their essence.[7]

The passages dealing with the relatively neutral relation of concealing and unconcealing as strife are so numerous that the list could be continued indefinitely. By 'neutral' I mean that there is no explicit emphasis on either the preserving or distorting character of that strife. A final passage from *On the Essence of Truth* might serve to conclude our documentation before going on to the question of concealing as distortion.

But because the full essence of truth contains the non-essence and above all holds sway as concealing, philosophy as a question into this truth is intrinsically discordant.[8]

We take leave of the relation of concealing and unconcealing as the strife of opposites, for now, and turn to concealing as a kind of distortion.

Concealing as Distortion

With the question of concealment as distortion, the question also arises as to who or what is "responsible" for this distortion. Heidegger sometimes allows that some of this responsibility lies with man; on the whole, however, he places the responsibility in the structure of being itself.

> We are familiar with concealment, whether in the form of things themselves and their connections concealing themselves before and for us, or in the form of ourselves planning, perpetrating and allowing a concealment, or in the form of both, a self-concealment of 'things' and a concealing of them mingling in us.[1]

But even this passage attributing some responsibility to the human being is deliberately ambiguous and inconclusive. The verbs describing the relation of human beings to concealment are so contradictory that they nearly cancel each other out. Planning (*vornehmen*) and perpetrating (*betreiben*) are fairly deliberate activities, whereas to consider allowing or permitting (*zulassen*) as willful activities is, at best, questionable.

A great deal of Heidegger's discussion of the 'opposite' of *aletheia* aims at showing that the common conception of that opposite as untruth or falsity must be derived from concealment. Without going into the ramifications of everything that Heidegger is saying about falsity (*pseudos*) as a modern interpretation of untruth as the mere opposite of correctness, we can state that the real opposite of *aletheia* embodying the same etymological root is not *pseudos*, but *lanthanomai*, which Heidegger translates as 'forgetting'. Forgetting is not some shortcoming of human beings but something more far-reaching and ominous in its implications.

It could be the case that the invisible cloud of forgottenness, the forgottenness of being, is spreading itself around the whole earth with its humanity, a forgottenness in which not this or that being, but being itself is forgotten.[2]

In order to experience this "forgottenness of being," thinking must somehow think being in its truth instead of representing being metaphysically as the being of beings, as the ground of beings. Since these two aspects, forgottenness of being and truth of being, are inseparable, we can reformulate this just as well, or perhaps even better, in reverse order: Only when we experience the *forgottenness* of being will we perhaps be able to think toward (*andenken*) the truth of being.

Forgetting, Heidegger says, was experienced by the Greeks as the occurrence of concealment. He is careful to emphasize that the common association with falsehood (*pseudos*) as the opposite of truth is by no means the only or even the primordial one. The question with regard to concealment is the same as our overall question with regard to truth. Obviously falsehood is in some sense detrimental to truth, preventing it from appearing as what it is. What, then, does 'forgetting' mean? Is it as clear that forgetting blocks and obscures truth as it is in the case of falsehood? Does forgetting possibly have a function similar to preserving and saving? We must look into the question of falsehood and forgetting as forms of concealing. Our basic question remains the same: What is the meaning of concealing?

Let us scrutinize *pseudos* first. Without going into all of the profound changes brought about by the romanization of Greece, we want to see what Heidegger makes of the original Greek sense of *pseudos,* which he comes to distinguish sharply from the Latin *falsum.*

Inquiring into the meaning of the false (*das Falsche*), Heidegger distinguishes various meanings of fake (a false Rembrandt), incorrect (a false statement), deceptive (a lie), wrong (the police got the wrong man), and cunning (some animals).

Trying to get back to the Greek meaning of *pseudos,* Heidegger distances it from any kind of subjectivity and places it back in the objective realm where it properly belongs. 'Subjective' and 'objective', of course, are modern terms that have no place in the epoch of the Greeks. Heidegger is using them because they are undeniably part of our present way of thinking; we are still burdened with them. *Pseudos* is essentially a form of *concealing;* it unconceals in a way that covers over.

Pseudos belongs in the essential realm of covering over, thus of a kind of concealing. But the covering over operative in *pseudos* is always at the same time an unveiling and showing and bringing to appearance.[3]

As an example for this covering over that at the same time lets something appear, Heidegger chooses the term 'pseudonym'. Kierkegaard's pseudonyms of Johannes de Silentio, Johannes Climacus and Anti-Climacus did not simply conceal the identity of their author but rather said something essential about him.

However, the interpretation, already latent with the Greeks and becoming decisive with the Romans and thereafter, of truth as *veritas* in the sense of correct statements blocks any possible understanding of what the Greeks in the beginning of Western philosophy thought as *aletheia* and *pseudos*.

Within the dominance of *veritas* and *rectitudo* how could there be or even try to be knowledge that *veritas* and *rectitudo* and *iustitia* not only do not really exhaust the incipient essence of truth, but can never exhaust it since they are what they are only as a consequence of *aletheia*. Even if Western metaphysics escalates the true to the Absolute Spirit of Hegel's metaphysics, even if 'the angels' and 'the holy ones' are claimed as 'the true,' the *essence* of truth has long since retreated from its beginning and that means at the same time from its *essential ground*, has fallen out of its beginning and is thus a discard.[4]

Whereas Heidegger's ultimate conclusion, at least in this lecture course, seems to be that distortion is not the only form of concealment, still there are many passages that undeniably emphasize the detrimental aspect of concealment. Speaking of the *polis*, Heidegger states that a prevalence of dis-essence (*Un-wesen*) and un-holiness (*Un-heil*) necessarily belongs to the abode of human beings.

This [dis-essence and un-holiness] belongs to the *polis* because all unconcealment of beings is in strife with concealment and thus also with distortion and disfigurement.[5]

Un-heil, here translated tentatively as "un-holiness," connotes the destruction of wholeness (*Heil*), the onset of ruin, disaster, definitely something gone wrong.

In an intriguing passage on the concluding myth of Plato's *Republic* which does indeed speak of *lethe* and the river from which those about to be reborn must drink, Heidegger discusses forgetting (*lethe*) as the occurrence of the concealment of beings. Whereas most interpretations of this passage, insofar as it is taken seriously and not passed off as a mere "myth," understand *lethe* to be the river itself, Heidegger states that *lethe* is neither the river not symbolized by the river; rather, *lethe* is a realm, a field. In so doing, he rejects the common interpretation of forgetting as a kind of lapse of memory and, correspondingly, of *anamnesis* as some kind of remembering of what was forgotten. Everything smacking of any kind of subjectivity, however ingrained it might be in our thinking, is totally out of place here. Originally, *lethe* had nothing to do with the human ability to retain or not to retain things in the mind. It is connected with a river because it and the river share the quality of being uncontainable.

> But what alone can be in the emptiness and desert of the field of the concealing that withdraws everything is a river because its waters correspond to the essence of the field since these waters withdraw from any being contained and thus bear the essence of this place of withdrawing concealing everywhere where they are consumed as a drink.[6]

The conclusion of this whole discussion of the final myth of *The Republic,* the myth of Er, suddenly reverses the meaning of *lethe* as emptiness and desert and, without further explanation or development, asserts its indispensable function for man.

> This withdrawing counteressence to unconcealing that 'withholds' unconcealment contains its essence in advance. The 'opposite' to *aletheia* is neither what is only contrary nor a mere lack nor the turning away of mere denial. *Lethe,* forgetting as withdrawing concealing, is that withdrawal through which alone the essence of *aletheia* can be kept and thus remain unforgotten and unforgettable.[7]

We turn now to concealment as a *process:* to the history of being as nihilism.

Concealment as Process: 5

Nihilism as the History of Being

In the fourth volume of the lecture course on Nietzsche, we find the following sentence:

> The essence of nihilism is the history in which there is nothing to being itself.[1]

Nihilism is conceived here as a process, as the history in which being itself is somehow eclipsed in favor of beings. This history is essentially the history of metaphysics, that is, of Western philosophy.

Nietzsche had distinguished between two kinds of nihilism: active and passive. As the terms 'active' and 'passive' indicate, passive nihilism represents our entrapment in the history of Platonism which posits a 'backworld' of eternal Forms judging and condemning our world of transiency and becoming as imperfect. Active nihilism is envisioned as the struggle out of passive nihilism; it is at least honest and liberating.

Instead of talking about Nietzsche's own distinction, Heidegger makes his own: that of appropriate or authentic nihilism and inappropriate or inauthentic nihilism. Nietzsche was the first thinker to understand nihilism as a historical process having its roots in Plato. Heidegger conceives Nietzsche's metaphysics as the ground of the *completion* of appropriate nihilism, but not of appropriate nihilism itself. Since for Nietzsche being was demoted to a mere value, he was unable to see that there is anything like a question of the essence of appropriate nihilism. Heidegger sees the ground of the completion of appropriate nihilism in the conception of beings as a whole as will. This conception has its explicit roots in Descartes (and, incidentally, in the medieval period in general). The nihilism already implicit in Plato now becomes explicit, heading for its completion in Nietzsche's conception of the will to power and of being as a mere value.

Appropriate nihilism (i.e., metaphysics) thinks beings on the basis of being, but it never thinks being as being, that is, being without regard to it as the ground of beings.

Of course, metaphysics acknowledges that beings are not without Being. But scarcely has it said so when it again transforms Being into a being, whether it be the supreme being in the sense of the first cause, whether it be the distinctive being in the sense of the subject of subjectivity, as the condition of the possibility of all objectivity, or whether, as a consequence of the coherence of both of these fundamental conditions of Being in beings, it be the determination of the supreme being as the Absolute in the sense of unconditioned subjectivity.[2]

Metaphysics seeks for something transcending everyday empirical reality. In this sense Heidegger began as a kind of metaphysician and never abandoned that search. But metaphysics inevitably turns this 'something' transcending everyday empirical reality into a being, albeit a special sort of being thought as the highest being that is the first cause. This Heidegger never did, not even in *Being and Time*. There, and in some subsequent works, he is still looking for conditions of possibility, but not in the form of a highest being. By consistently stating from the outset that being was finite, Heidegger never trod the path of traditional metaphysics. That metaphysics was somehow suspect to him from the very beginning is evident in the fact that the word is almost always set in quotation marks in *Being and Time*. What was more difficult for him to relinquish was the idea of grounding and making possible.

As Heidegger pointed out in "The Onto-theo-logical Constitution of Metaphysics," the difficulty lies in the nature of Western language, which appears to be branded by the structure of metaphysics. Certainly Aristotle's categories pretty much determine our grammar; they pin down the kinds of things we can say about things. We can speak about nouns, verbs, adjectives, adverbs, and so forth. In *Being and Time,* Heidegger is relying heavily on prepositions as the connecting tissue *between* things, and his thinking has always been expressly verbal, from the word *being* down to the term 'essence' or 'presencing' (*Wesen*). Yet it seems that language, even to a far lesser extent Eastern languages, has its distinct limitations. In this regard, one might say that Wittgenstein was more radically consistent than Heidegger. Unlike Heidegger, he did not try to speak of that which cannot be spoken about.

However, the main reason that metaphysics is unable to think being is that being itself remains absent. It is not the case that metaphysical thinking neglects or refuses to think being other than as a being, albeit a special and highest being.

> In the meantime it has become clearer that Being itself occurs essentially as the unconcealment in which the being comes to presence. Unconcealment, however, remains concealed as such. With reference to itself, unconcealment as such keeps away, keeps to itself. *The matter stands with the concealment of the essence of unconcealment. It stands with the concealment of Being as such. Being itself stays away.*[3]

Being itself presences as the unconcealment in which beings become present. But this unconcealment itself remains concealed. Here concealment is in no way what preserves unconcealment, but rather the privative form of being solely available to us: absence, remaining absent. What makes everything still more difficult is the fact that this concealment conceals itself so that thinking is not even aware that there is any concealment involved here at all. This is all that we have of being, its remaining absent. Being is not off somewhere, intact and, as it were, waiting in the wings. The remaining absent of being is the only way in which being is accessible to us now.

> Is concealing simply a veiling or is it at the same time a storing away and preserving?[4]

This question is left open. It is perhaps not answerable in terms of a simple either-or. But this much is clear. Metaphysics is the history of the unconcealment of beings and the withdrawal of being. This is appropriate nihilism. Being itself withdraws and remains absent. This remaining absent is the way that being 'is'. Being is not off somewhere, separate, by itself, but 'is' here in the form of remaining absent. What 'is', or presences, in remaining absent is the relation to something like a place from which remaining absent stays away. In this place unconcealment remains absent and concealment remains.

> But the staying away of unconcealment and the staying of concealment do not subsequently search about for an abode;

rather, the abode occurs essentially with them as the advent that Being itself is. The advent is in itself the advent of their abode. The locale of the place of Being as such is Being itself.[5]

This locale is the essence of man, not insofar as he represents beings, but insofar as he stands ecstatically in this locale.

As the relation to Being, whether it is to the being as such or to Being itself, ecstative inherence in the openness of the locale of Being is the essence of thinking.[6]

But the possibility of realizing the relation to being as being itself has not been followed by metaphysical thinking. This thinking brings being in the form of beings to language; it does not heed, or correspond to, the withdrawal of being.

Rather, it happens not only that Being as such stays away, but that its default is thoughtlessly misplaced and suppressed by thinking.[7]

The fact that being remains absent constitutes true or appropriate nihilism. Inappropriate nihilism occurs when metaphysical thinking omits and leaves out the remaining absent of being and, beyond that, is totally unaware that it is leaving anything out. To give a questionable, ontic example, to ignore someone totally is not even to be aware that you are ignoring him.
    The distinction 'appropriate–inappropriate', 'authentic–inauthentic', of course, has its roots in *Being and Time* as ways of being of *Da-sein.* In *Being and Time,* we find contradictory statements regarding the relation of these two ways of being. Most frequently, Heidegger says that authenticity is a modification of inauthenticity, but in a couple of passages, he states the opposite. A remnant of that problem is still present in the attempt to determine the relation of appropriate and inappropriate nihilism.

The full essence of nihilism is the original unity of its appropriateness and inappropriateness.[8]

This would appear to mean that appropriate nihilism as the remaining absent of being is completed by the leaving out of this remaining absent. Inappropriate nihilism, then, also leaves out this leaving out so that there is truly 'nothing' at all with regard to being.

Behind all of this discussion, of course, lurks the question of what we can "do" about this situation. For Heidegger, to wish to overcome nihilism would be the most fatal attitude of all. Nihilism, after all, has to do with being itself, not merely with beings. Directly willing to overcome nihilism is totally out of place; we can force nothing here. In fact, it is just this activity of forcing, controlling, and manipulating that constitutes the problem. Technology and the will to will are hardly the solution to our dilemma. What, then, can we do?

> But how would it be if the overcoming did not directly assail the default of Being itself and stopped trying to measure up to Being itself, while advancing upon the omission of the default? The omission, in the form of metaphysics, is the work of human thought. Would it not be possible for thought to advance upon its own failure, namely the failure to think Being itself in its unconcealment?[9]

We must become aware of the fact that we are neglecting and leaving out something. We must experience the inappropriate aspect of nihilism. But this could become possible only if we come face to face with the appropriate aspect, with the remaining absent of being itself. Since being itself brings about thinking's leaving out of being's remaining absent, no *direct* action or willing on our part can do anything but worsen the situation. The word *direct* or *immediate,* *(unmittelbar)* is crucial here. Only when being itself directly makes a move encouraging the essence of man to experience, not represent, the remaining absent of being's unconcealment as an arrival of being itself can things begin to turn around. Then remaining absent would arrive, would be unconcealed.

> Instead of such overcoming, only one thing is necessary, namely, that thinking, encouraged by Being itself, simply think to encounter Being in its default as such. Such thinking to encounter rests primarily on the recognition that *Being itself withdraws, but that as this withdrawing Being is precisely the relationship that claims the essence of man, as the abode of its (Being's) advent.*[10]

Thinking to encounter, thinking toward (*entgegendenken*), does not leave out the remaining absent of being, nor does it attempt to control and manipulate that remaining absent. Thinking to encounter follows being's withdrawal by letting it go, and by itself remaining behind. Where does this leave thinking? Such thinking takes the step back out of metaphysical thinking into the realm long since granted to thinking by being itself. There, thinking experiences the arrival of being's remaining absent.

> The inauthenticity in the essence of nihilism is the history of omission; that is, of the concealing of the promise. Granted, however, that Being itself saves itself in its default, then the history of the omission of the default is precisely the preservation of that self-saving of Being itself.[11]

Appropriate thinking toward being's remaining absent experiences being's promising of itself. It glimpses the possibility of a different "relation" to being. For the history of the leaving out of remaining absent is the preservation of being's saving itself. Being saves itself and promises itself to man.

A word about the term 'relation' with regard to man and being. This is a problem that does not just crop up now but pervades all of Heidegger's writings. It becomes more and more pressing and critical in the later writings as he casts about for ways to express what he is trying to say. I can only touch upon this question for now and hope to get back to it.

The relation between man and being is one of identity and one of difference. Both factors, identity and difference, are absolutely central to this relation and must be thought in a nonontotheological way. Thus, Heidegger will always maintain a difference between being and beings but will eventually relinquish the important term 'ontological difference'.

> If the ontological difference here appearing is the most dangerous matter for thinking, it is because thinking always represents being in the horizon of metaphysics as a being.[12]

Insofar as being can never be thought as any being whatsoever, the element of difference will always be maintained. The problem is that metaphysics and ontology will inevitably represent being as a being.

> We will not succeed in thinking Appropriation with the concepts of being and history of being; . . . Together with being, the ontological difference also disappears. By way of anticipation we would also have to regard the continued reference to

the ontological difference from 1927 to 1936 as a necessary
blind alley (*Holzweg*).[13]

Heidegger's grammatical attempts to "locate" being, what he
calls a "topology of being," move from a verbal to a prepositional emphasis and finally to something like a dimension, region, or realm.
His continual rejection of being thought as *constant presence* led
him to embrace the nothing as the negation of constant presence. I
shall come back to the question of the nothing later.

The second factor essential to the relation of man and being,
that of identity, also needs to be rethought in a nonontotheological
way. Heidegger's way of rethinking identity as Appropriation is expressed in the phrase "belonging together." Using one of his favorite
devices, he attempts to show the movement from a metaphysically
thought identity to a nonmetaphysical one. That device consists of a
shift of intonation.

If we think of belonging *together* in the customary way, the
meaning of belonging is determined by the word together,
that is, by its unity. In that case, 'to belong' means as much as:
to be assigned and placed into the order of a 'together,' established in the unity of a manifold, combined into, the unity of a
system, mediated by the unifying center of an authoritative
synthesis. Philosophy represents this belonging together as
nexus and *connexio*.

However, belonging together can also be thought of as *belonging* together. This means: the 'together' is now determined
by the belonging. Of course, we must still ask what 'belong'
means in that case, and how its peculiar 'together' is determined only in its terms. The answer to these questions is
closer to us than we imagine, but it is not obvious. Enough for
now that this reference makes us note the possibility of no
longer representing belonging together in terms of the unity of
the together, but rather of experiencing this together in terms
of belonging.[14]

The unity of the together is the metaphysically conceived
framework into which man and being are to be fitted. The *together*
consists of an objectively present order of a static framework containing man and being, also conceived as objectively present, geared
to each other. *Belonging*, which is far more difficult to delineate, ob-
viates all associations with objective presence and static entities.

Obviously I cannot exhaust this most difficult and absolutely central issue of relation with these cursory remarks. I shall return to this question later.

> That which according to its essence preservingly conceals, and thus remains concealed in its essence and entirely hidden, though nonetheless it somehow appears, is in itself what we call *the mystery*. In the inauthenticity of the essence of nihilism, the mystery of the promise occurs, in which form Being is Itself, in that it saves itself as such. The history of the secret, the mystery itself in its history, is the essence of the history of the omission of the default of Being. The omission of Being itself in the thought of beings as such is the history of the unconcealment of beings as such. That history is metaphysics.[15]

The word *mystery* names concealing and unconcealing together. Somehow, something makes itself known; otherwise we could not even speak of a mystery. On the other hand, we do not, and essentially cannot, know what the mystery is, presumably because it is not a 'what' at all.

In *Gelassenheit*, Heidegger speaks of the openness for the mystery and the releasement toward things.

> What shows itself in such a way and at the same time withdraws is a fundamental trait of what we call the mystery. I call the posture by dint of which we keep ourselves open for the meaning hidden in the technological world: the openness for the mystery. The releasement toward things and the openness for the mystery belong together. They grant us the possibility of dwelling in the world in a completely different way. They promise us a new ground and soil on which we can stand and persist in the technological world unendangered by that world.[16]

Heidegger frequently cites the lines from Hölderlin: "But where there is danger, there grows also what saves." The danger has to do with the essence of technology, framing, a subject we shall have to return to at the end of this chapter. This passage just quoted names the possibility of a way of dwelling in the world that is unendangered.

Thinking abandons the pure 'metaphysics of metaphysics' by taking the step back, back from the omission of Being in its default. In the step *back,* thinking has already set out on the path of thinking to *encounter* Being itself in its self-withdrawal. That self-withdrawal, as the self-withdrawal of Being, still remains a mode of Being—an advent. By thinking to encounter Being itself, thinking no longer omits Being, but admits it: admits it *into* the originary, revealing unconcealment of Being, which is Being itself.[17]

We conclude this discussion of nihilism as found in the fourth Nietzsche volume by taking a look at what Heidegger calls the need of needlessness. He also characterizes it as the separating of appropriate and inappropriate nihilism. The central term for this, which does not appear in this context, is 'Framing' (*Gestell*).

Of course, the difference between inauthenticity and authenticity which reigns in the essential unity of nihilism could diverge into the most extreme disjunction of inauthentic from authentic. Then, in keeping with its own essence, the essential unity of nihilism would have to conceal itself in what is most extreme.[18]

Inauthentic or inappropriate nihilism, which belongs in an essential unity together with appropriate nihilism, can, or perhaps even has a tendency to, strike off on its own. This possibility explains the destructive aspect of nihilism.

In this way, the inauthenticity in nihilism reaches absolute predominance, behind which the authenticity—and along with authenticity and its relation to inauthenticity the essence of nihilism—remains submerged in the inaccessible and unthinkable. In our epoch of the history of Being, only the consequences of the predominance of the inauthenticity in nihilism takes effect, although never as consequences, but simply as nihilism itself. Nihilism therefore reveals only destructive features.[19]

One might conclude from this passage that ours is an epoch in the history of Being where inauthentic or inappropriate nihilism has become predominant. Inappropriate nihilism is characterized by a leaving out of being's remaining absent. Being needs an abode, an abode for its remaining absent since that is the way being 'is' right now. But man does not pay any heed to this need of being; he is not aware of any need at all. It seems to him that being is without need.

But the needlessness that establishes itself as the dominion of metaphysics brings Being itself to the utmost limit of its need. Need is not merely what compels in the sense of the unyielding claim that occupies an abode by using it as the unconcealment of the advent; that is, by letting it unfold essentially as the truth of Being. The relentlessness of its usage extends so far in the default of its unconcealment that the abode of Being—that is, the essence of man—is omitted; man is threatened with the annihilation of his essence, and Being itself is endangered in the usage of its abode.[20]

Being needs and uses (*braucht*) man as the abode for its arrival. Man must realize that there is a need at stake here. He can best do this by transforming his thinking, by thinking toward (*entgegendenken, andenken*) being instead of representing it metaphysically as a being.

Framing   6

As a conclusion to these sections on concealment, we need to say something about Framing (*das Gestell*). Framing comes out of the essence of technology. It comprises the nongeneric unity of activities involving the verb *stellen,* to place, put, set: *stellen* (challenge), *vorstellen* (represent), *ent-stellen* (disfigure), *nach-stellen* (to be after someone). One might say that Framing is the diametric opposite of *Gelassenheit,* releasement. Whereas releasement lets things be, Framing does not let anything be at all; it manipulates everything. The important thing about modern technology is not that it is a product of man nor that it is a means to an end. Modern technology is a mode of revealing (*Entbergen*). It challenges nature to yield energy that can be stored. Framing challenges man to reveal the real as standing-reserve (*Bestand*).

> The essence of technology lies in enframing. Its hidden sway belongs within destining. Since destining at any given time starts man on a way of revealing, man, thus underway, is continually approaching the brink of the possibility of pursuing and pushing forward nothing but what is revealed in ordering, and of deriving all his standards on this basis. Through this the other possibility is blocked, that man might be admitted more and sooner and ever more primally to the essence of what is unconcealed and to its unconcealment, in order that he might experience as his essence the requisite belonging to revealing.
>
> Placed between these possibilities, man is endangered by destining. The destiny revealing is as such, in every one of its modes, and therefore necessarily, *danger.*[1]

The first possibility, that of Framing, threatens to push man to the extreme of perpetrating only what is revealed in the mode of ordering and of admitting as real only that which fits into this mode.

The other possibility, which moves in the direction of Appropriation, is for man to be admitted to what is unconcealed and its unconcealment, and to experience the fact that he belongs to this revealing. If man can *belong* to revealing, we are moving in the direction of Appropriation or belonging-together. In the mode of Framing, man does not belong to anything but dissolves into being the uncanny orderer of the standing-reserve.

What is the danger? It lies with revealing. In perpetrating the ordering of standing-reserve, man comes to believe that everything he encounters is under the control of his domination. Meanwhile, man himself is rapidly approaching the point where he will be nothing more than an occurrence of standing-reserve. One would like to use the more familiar expression "cog in a wheel," but that has become inappropriate since we are no longer dealing with objects of any sort, with something over against us, but rather with stored-up energies.

> But enframing does not simply endanger man in his relationship to himself and to everything that is. As a destining, it banishes man into that kind of revealing that is an ordering. Above all, enframing conceals that revealing which, in the sense of *poiesis,* lets what presences come forth into appearance. Where this ordering holds sway, it drives out every other possibility of revealing. As compared with that other revealing, the setting-upon that challenges forth thrusts man into a relation to whatever is that is at once antithetical and rigorously ordered. Where enframing holds sway, regulating and securing of the standing-reserve mark all revealing. They no longer even let their own fundamental characteristic appear, namely, this revealing as such. Thus the challenging-enframing not only conceals a former way of revealing, bringing forth, but it conceals revealing itself and with it that wherein unconcealment, i.e., truth, comes to pass. Enframing blocks the shining-forth and holding sway of truth.[2]

Here we have a most remarkable situation. Framing is a mode of revealing that blocks revealing itself. Since everything that occurs, including modern technology, is some kind of revealing—otherwise it would not be—we have to allow for the possibility that there be a kind of revealing that conceals. To make things even stranger and uncannier, man thinks that he is the inventor and originator of all this. He thinks himself to be "the lord of the earth" (Nietzsche), whereas in truth he is nothing but the extraordinary puppet of Framing. He fails to hear that he is being addressed by a claim. Technology is a destining; it is never produced by man. But in an age where almost no one believes in anything transcending man, it is small wonder that we are unable to hear that we are being addressed. Thus, we would appear to be irretrievably stuck in the destining of Framing precisely because we do not realize that it is a destining, something sent to us.

> The essence of technology is in a lofty sense ambiguous. Such ambiguity points to the mystery of all revealing, i.e., of truth. On the one hand, enframing challenges forth into the frenzied-ness of ordering that blocks every view into the coming-to-pass of revealing and so radically endangers the relation to the essence of truth. On the other hand, enframing comes to pass for its part in the granting that lets man endure—as yet inexperienced, but perhaps more experienced in the future—that he may be the one who is needed and used for the safekeeping of the essence of truth. Thus does the arising of the saving power appear.[3]

The question prevalent in Heidegger's later writings is whether mankind gets indefinitely entrenched in Framing or whether a more appropriate relation of man and being might come about in the form of Appropriation. This question never gets answered. We don't know.

> The completion of metaphysics sets beings in the abandonment of Being. Being's abandonment of beings is the last reflection of Being as the concealment of unconcealment in which all beings of any sort as such are able to appear. Being's abandonment contains the undecided factor of whether beings persist in their precedence. In the future, this means the question of whether beings undermine and uproot every possibility of the origin in Being, and thus continue to be busy with beings, but also move towards the desolation that does not destroy, but rather chokes what is primal in organizing and ordering. Being's abandonment contains the undecided factor of whether the unconcealment of this concealment, and thus the more primal Origin, is already opening up in this abandonment as an extreme of the concealment of Being.[4]

Insofar as it is possible, we shall try to discuss Framing by itself, leaving a discussion of Appropriation for the sections on the Open (*das Offene*) and the opening or clearing (*die Lichtung*).

'Framing', 'technology', and 'the completion of metaphysics' are all different names for the same matter.

In Framing man is challenged to relate himself to exploitation and depletion accordingly. The relation to exploitation and depletion forces man to *be* in this relation. Man does not have technology under control. He is its toy. In this situation total forgottenness of being reigns, total concealment of being. Cybernetics becomes the ersatz for philosophy and poetry. Political science, sociology and psychology become predominant, subjects that no longer have the slightest relation to their foundations. In this respect, modern man is the slave of the forgottenness of being.[5]

In reading this passage, it is difficult to accept completely Heidegger's insistence that there is nothing negative about technology and Framing. But in addition to this insistence, he asserts even more frequently that Framing is not necessarily a permanent or stable situation. It is a sort of crossroads, a situation where things can go one way or the other. Framing could turn out to be a preliminary form of Appropriation.

The Open, the Opening   7

The fourth directive (p. 000) for thinking *aletheia*, truth, points to the Open (*das Offene*) and the opening or clearing (*die Lichtung*). We must begin our attempt to understand what Heidegger means with these words by seeing how they differ from the Open in Rilke. The Open, *das Offene*, is a fundamental word in Rilke's poetry, particularly in the eighth of the *Duino Elegies*. In at least two passages—in the Parmenides lecture course we have been discussing and in the essay "What are Poets For?"—Heidegger is careful emphatically to differentiate what Rilke says poetically about the Open from what he, Heidegger, thinks as the Open. Whereas the poet appears to be able to do things the thinker cannot, namely, to *name* and not just to *say*,[1] the poet Rilke, according to Heidegger, is not privy to such a distinctive possibility. Rather, Rilke is trapped in the popular biological metaphysics of the late nineteenth century. The background of Rilke's poetry is the spirit of Schopenhauer, mediated by Nietzsche and the doctrines of psychoanalysis. Let it be noted that I am not taking a stand on whether I agree or disagree with Heidegger's assessment of Rilke. I am trying only to see how Heidegger differentiates his understanding of the Open from that of Rilke. There is clearly a marked difference.

    The Parmenides lecture course is from the years 1942–43. By this time, Heidegger had given up the ontological difference as something irretrievably branded by metaphysics. But he never gave up *a difference* between being and beings. To do this would mean either flattening being down to the level of a being or else demoting being to the level of a mere concept. When this happens, being by no means *becomes* a mere being or even a mere concept but remains "operative" in an uncanny, inappropriate way. Without being, 'there is' nothing at all (in the sense of the nugatory nothing, *das nichtige Nichts*). Thus, when the difference between being and beings disappears, being remains in the midst of beings as a whole. In so doing, it covers itself over as what has withdrawn and closed itself off.

Here we have a double concealment. Being, which is the opening Open, has withdrawn and closed itself off and remains in the midst of beings as a whole covering over the fact that it has withdrawn. This is the clearest statement that I am able to make about this by no means simple and transparent situation.

According to Heidegger, Rilke is trapped in this situation where the withdrawing of the difference between being and beings is covered over. For this reason he remains in metaphysics, unlike Hölderlin.

> This unlimited progression from being to being of the succession and permeation of beings is supposed to be 'being.' This unlimited progression from being to being then points to 'the Open' in the sense in which we speak of the 'open sea' when the high seas are attained in which all the limits of land have disappeared.
>
> This is how Rilke understands 'the Open' in his eighth Duino Elegy. 'The Open' is for him constant progression, on the part of beings themselves and traversed by them alone, of beings to beings within beings.[2]

Rilke's Open is conceived on the exclusive level of beings without regard to any other 'dimension'. The Open is thus not beings themselves, but the constant possibility of moving from one being to another without impediment.

> 'Infinitely' here means both 'endlessly,' without stopping at a limit, and also 'in the whole.' 'Arising,' of course, does not signify *phuein* thought in the Greek way, but rather that 'arising' through which, like the melting piece of sugar in water, what arises dissipates and blends itself in the whole of air and all cosmic relations.[3]

In the poem in question, Rilke is speaking about the difference between man and other living beings. Since man as subject represents everything to himself as object, he remains ever a spectator, turned toward objects and never getting beyond them to the Open. But the animal neither represents things to itself nor is it 'bent back upon itself' (re-flected) in the mode of self-consciousness. The animal, the creature, sees the Open with all eyes. All that we know of the Open and what is Outside we know solely from the countenance of the animal.

For the animal's sight our eyes are 'traps' into which it falls and in which it remains caught. 'Traps' that set upon, close off and hinder the Open. The phrase 'open seas' best tells us what this means. The open seas are reached when all land boundaries have disappeared. The Open is the lack and absence of limits and boundaries, the objectless, but conceived not as a fault, but as the primordial whole of what is real into which the creature is immediately admitted and freed.[4]

Rilke conceived the animal's way of seeing as free of objectifying and categorizing. "The Open" means a space free of all limits and conceptual overlay. In contrast to man, the animal has direct and immediate access to this Open. But Heidegger traces this assessment of the privileged situation of the animal back to the nineteenth century preference for the unconscious as opposed to the conscious. While he has a strong sense of the mysteriousness and inscrutability of the animal, Heidegger is far from seeing anything superior to man in this mysteriousness. In the lecture course *Basic Concepts of Metaphysics,* he states that the animal is world-poor (*weltarm*) in contrast to man who is world-forming (*welt-bildend*). Heidegger is critical of Rilke for confounding the realms of the animal and the human. He finds the concept of the animal to be basically anthropomorphic and the concept of the human being to be exclusively biologically oriented. For Heidegger, the Open cannot be a space merely free of human representation and categorization accessible directly only to the animal as a privileged being.

Between that which Rilke calls 'the Open' and the Open in the sense of the unconcealment of beings there yawns a gap. The 'Open' presencing in *aletheia* first lets beings arise and presence as beings. Only man sees this Open. More precisely, man initially and for the most part looks into this Open by everywhere and constantly relating to beings, whether these beings are encountered in a Greek fashion as what presences in arising, in a Christian fashion as created beings, or in a modern fashion as objects. Relating to beings, man looks into the Open in advance by standing in the opening and opened project of being. Without the Open as which being itself presences, beings could neither be unconcealed nor concealed.[5]

Here the Open is brought in close proximity to the world and to the 'as'—structure of human perceiving.

No movability nor excitability of plant and animal ever bring the living being into the free in such a way that what is excited could ever let what is stimulating just 'be' what it as stimulating is, let alone what it is before stimulating and without this.[6]

The plant or animal simply absorbs a stimulus immediately without the possibility of realizing what it is that is stimulating them or what that could be apart from its activity of stimulating.

These passages contain one of the rare instances where the Open is prior to either concealment or unconcealment. In this case, concealment is not the constitutive counterpart to unconcealment; rather, both concealment and unconcealment presuppose the Open, a cleared, free space in which anything at all can be.

In "What Are Poets For?" Heidegger assembles many of Rilke's names for being. These names, which, in keeping with the greater richness and freedom of poetry, are more concrete and thought-provoking than the worn-out and used-up term 'being', read as follows: the venture, the unheard-of center, the pure draft, the other draft, the gravity of the pure forces, the eternal playmate, Nature, Life, the Open.

Rilke likes to use the term 'the Open' to designate the whole draft to which all beings, as ventured beings, are given over. It is another basic word in his poetry. In Rilke's language, 'open' means something that does not block off. It does not block off because it does not set bounds. It does not set bounds because it is in itself without all bounds. The Open is the great whole that is unbounded.[7]

Here Heidegger is placing Rilke's Open in the Christian context of the in-finite, that which has no bounds or limits. This is an extremely positive conception. Heidegger, however, is far closer to the Greek view of infinity as a kind of nothingness, a view first explicitly brought out by Nietzsche, in *The Birth of Tragedy*, when he said that the Greeks had a horror of infinity. What is has limits (*peras*). What does not have limits is not.

What Rilke designates by this term (the Open) is not in any way defined by openness in the sense of the unconcealedness of beings that lets beings as such be present. If we attempted to interpret what Rilke has in mind as the open in the sense of unconcealedness and what is unconcealed, we would have to say: what Rilke experiences as the Open is precisely what is closed up, unlightened, which draws on in boundlessness, so that it is incapable of encountering anything unusual, or indeed anything at all.[8]

For Rilke, plant and animal are admitted into the Open. They are *in* the world. By contrast, man represents; he places everything over against himself and thus stands *before* the world, not in it. Man is debarred from admittance into the Open because he would objectify it and twist it around to stand over against him. Man's activities of representing and, above all, of producing impede the drawing of the pure draft. Thus man stands before the obstructed Open, unshielded.

From here, Heidegger goes into an elaborate discussion of the will to will and technology, a discussion that has some basis in what Rilke is saying but that goes beyond it. What interests us is the difference between the Open in Rilke's and Heidegger's conceptions. How can Heidegger say that Rilke's Open is precisely what is closed off, unlightened?

That is an extremely difficult question. Both thinkers are interested in varying degrees of consciousness, a concern Heidegger traces back to Leibniz. Plant, animal, man, and, for Rilke, the angel all have different levels of consciousness. For Rilke, what is distinctive about man, his reason, is what excludes him from the Open and leaves him unshielded. Unshieldedness consists in separation and parting, not in parting *from,* but in parting *against* the Open.

But this self-assertion not only places man outside all care or protection; the imposition of the objectifying of the world destroys ever more resolutely the very possibility of protection. By building the world up technologically as an object, man deliberately and completely blocks his path, already obstructed, into the Open. Self-assertive man, whether or not he knows and wills it as an individual, is the functionary of technology. Not only does he face the Open from outside it; he even turns his back upon the 'pure draft' by objectifying the world. Man sets himself apart from the pure draft. The man of the age of technology, by this parting, opposes himself to the Open. This parting is not a parting *from,* it is a parting *against.*[9]

All of this self-assertion and willing that excludes man from the Open by making it an object and twisting it around toward him is by no means any kind of free activity. This willing is itself willed without man having any awareness that he is being willed. He is being willed by the will to will, the last epoch of subjectivity and metaphysics, synonymous with technology. Actually, there appears to be no such thing as 'free will' in Heidegger; all willing belongs to the epoch of the completion of metaphysics. Willing is not so much fatalistically determined as it is somehow *compelled* because it does not realize what is going on. Could it realize that it is being used as a tool by the will to will, willing could perhaps free itself. It is not a matter of coincidence that Heidegger gives a detailed and insightful analysis of Nietzsche's will and its revenge against the 'it was'.

But there is a sense of will other than self-assertion. That is will in the sense of being willing (*willig*), of going along with the venture of being.

> Like all beings, we are in being only by being ventured in the venture of Being. But because, as the beings who will, we go with the venture, we are more venturesome and thus sooner exposed to danger. When man entrenches himself in purposeful self-assertion, and by means of absolute objectification installs himself in the parting against the Open, then he himself promotes his own unshieldedness. But the daring which is more venturesome creates a safety for us.[10]

We are unshielded, unprotected. But our daring which is more venturesome creates a safety net for us. Heidegger takes safety and security in the literal sense of *sine cura,* without care.

> The caring here has the character of purposeful self-assertion by the ways and means of unconditional production. We are without such care only when we do not establish our nature exclusively within the precinct of production and procurement of things that can be utilized and defended. We are secure only where we neither reckon with the unprotected nor count on a defense erected within willing. A safety exists only outside the objectifying turning away from the Open, 'outside all caring,' outside the parting against the pure draft.[11]

Our being willing, which is stronger than any willing in the sense of self-assertion, brings about a security for us in the Open. This different sense of willing as being willing transmutes our unshieldedness, which consists in parting against the Open, into a turning towards the Open and into it. Thus a conversion, in the literal sense of a turning around, of our unshieldedness comes about and we are sheltered within the Open. How does this concretely come about? By a profound transformation of our consciousness. Calculating consciousness, which no longer is in touch with anything immediately seen, with sensible intuition, must become the true interior of the heart's space. It is the heart, rather than calculating reason, that brings about the inward conversion to the Open. We are able to know of this inward conversion, the transmutation of what is visible in representation into what is an invisible of the heart, through the being who has already accomplished this: the Angel.

In his letter of November 13, 1925 Rilke writes: "The Angel of the *Elegies* is that creature in whom the transmutation of the visible into the invisible, which we achieve, seems already accomplished. The Angel of the *Elegies* is that being who assures the recognition of a higher order of reality in the invisible."[12]

It is the poet who helps to achieve the transition from the realm of calculating reason to the Angel.

The more venturesome are the poets, but poets whose song turns our unprotected being into the Open. Because they convert the parting against the Open and inwardly recall its unwholesomeness into a sound whole, these poets sing the healing whole in the midst of the unholy. The recalling conversion has already overtaken the parting against the Open. It is 'ahead of all parting' and outlives everything objective within the world's inner space of the heart.[13]

To conclude this consideration of the Open in Rilke as compared with Heidegger, we return to the statement that Rilke's Open is precisely what is closed up, unlightened, which draws on in boundlessness, so that it is incapable of encountering anything at all. It would appear that Heidegger thinks of Rilke's Open as some sort of 'bad infinite' within which nothing can be encountered, nothing can happen. But on what basis he can say that Rilke's Open is closed up is not immediately clear, nor does he offer any further clarification.

The Open in Heidegger's Conception   8

We turn now to Heidegger's own conception of the Open and the Opening. In contrast to Rilke's understanding of the Open, Heidegger claims that his conception is no longer metaphysical, no longer within the realm of subjectivity.

> Indeed, through the immediately preceding references, i.e., in regard to the essential relation of *aletheia* to *lethe* (to withdrawing concealing), an *incipient essential factor of aletheia* shows itself which we have not named and which is by no means expressed by the translation 'unconcealment,' at least not as long as we think 'unconcealment' indefinitely in a loose sense only as the lack and removal of concealment.[1]

Heidegger begins his discussion of the fourth directive by insisting that unconcealment is not just the removal of concealment. He now emphasizes the verb *reveal: entbergen,* which lacks the prefix *ver-.* This removes the element of totally concealing and leaves us with the verb *bergen,* to shelter, harbor, keep safe, plus the prefix *ent-. Unverborgenheit* now means the mere removal of concealment, whereas *Entbergen* means something different.

> What is unconcealed is incipiently what has been saved in revealing from withdrawing concealment, and thus sheltered and as such what has not departed (*das Unentgangene*). What is unconcealed is not what presences indefinitely, from which the wrapping of concealment has fallen away. What is unconcealed is what overcomes absence, over which a withdrawing concealing no longer reigns. . . . What is unconcealed is what has entered into the rest of pure appearing and outward appearance. What is unconcealed is what is thus sheltered.[2]

In a passage quoted earlier, Heidegger interprets the prefix *ent-,* which usually means something like 'against', to mean a kind of intensification of the following verb rather than an opposition. The emphasis on concealment is replaced by sheltering and safe-keeping.

> Rather, *Ent*bergen is at the same time Ent*bergen,* like enflaming which does not remove the flames, but brings them to their essence. . . . *'Ent-bergen'* now means at the same time to *bring to a shelter:* namely, to *preserve* what is unconcealed in unconcealment.[3]

To summarize and clarify, we have now discovered the following possibilities in the conception of 'truth'. I repeat Heidegger's four directives as he envisions them and shall then try to map out where we now stand. Heidegger's four directives:

1. Un-*concealment*
    a) covering over
    b) preserving
2. *Un*-concealment—the removal of concealment—
    the question of strife
3. The question of the opposite of truth: concealment and falsehood
4. The Open

Keeping all of these possibilities in mind, we are trying for more clarification, which in this case results in different emphases of these possibilities. Again, trying to summarize and clarify, we have:

1. Unconcealment as preservation
2. Strife between concealment and unconcealment
3. Concealment as distortion
4. The Open

The fact that in Heidegger's discussion of the fourth directive, the Open, the first directive reappears should give us pause. We should consider the question of whether the factor of preservation and sheltering might not be indigenous to truth as the Open or the Opening. If this were the case, then the division between concealment as sheltering and as a distortion would become more sharply defined. Heidegger himself asks this question in one passage, only to let it fall in the pursuit of other matters.

But if in our perspective on *lethe* the *fundamental trait of safe-keeping* appears in the essence of revealing (*Entbergung*) and if this safekeeping shelters what it has to shelter and save in unconcealment, the question arises of what unconcealment itself might be so that it can hold sway as what shelters and saves.[4]

Heidegger is somehow very cautious and tentative in speaking about the fourth directive, the Open. We must be very careful to search out the few statements that he makes and not allow ourselves to be sidetracked when he goes off into other favorite important issues, such as the history of subjectivity. It is not that these issues are not of paramount importance; but they never lead back to the question of the Open.

What we are trying to get an essential look at through the fourth directive belongs *still more incipiently* to the essence of *aletheia* than the counteressence with its manifoldness that we have mentioned up to now.[5]

Here Heidegger has stated that the Open is more primordial than the conception of truth as strife, as the struggle between concealment and unconcealment. He gives us the analogy of brightness, light, and transparency. We everywhere see things; we utterly fail to perceive what makes this seeing possible: openedness and transparency. We might add an analogy with air. We go about our everyday affairs completely oblivious to something without which we could not exist for one minute: the air that we are breathing. We are breathing every second of our lives, and yet most of us are totally unaware of this.

The Open reigns in the essence of unconcealment. On first hearing this word we think of what is not closed off, thus opened. Thought in this way, the Open shows itself as a consequence of opening and revealing. It remains undecided whether the Open, instead of being only a consequence, must not be the essential ground of revealing that first gives the possibility of unconcealment.[6]

One of the reasons, if not *the* reason, that Heidegger is so reticent in speaking about the Open is that, as he himself admits, the Greeks did not explicitly speak of it.

The essence of unconcealment directs us to the Open and openness. But what is this? Here the Greeks are silent. We remain without support and help when it becomes necessary to think about the essence of the Open reigning in *aletheia*. This thinking is particularly alienating for common opinion because it shows underway that the Open is by no means only the result and consequence of revealing, but the ground and essential beginning of unconcealment.[7]

Another name for the Open that Heidegger introduces is 'the free' or 'freedom'. Although freedom is a basic conception in his thinking, it does not maintain the central place that Heidegger accords it here, presumably because it, almost to a greater degree than concepts such as forgetting, is almost impossible to separate from anthropomorphic conceptions. A notable exception is to be found in the lecture course *Schelling on Human Freedom,* where Heidegger tackles not only the question of freedom but also its inevitable companion, the problem of evil.

Heidegger retains, in *Parmenides,* the conception of the free in the following passage after having distanced it from the by now hackneyed question of human free will.

> The free is the guarantee, the sheltering place for the being of beings. As the free, the Open is what shelters and the sheltering of being. It is true that one rather thinks the Open and free and wide as the opportunity of dispersal, of scattering and strewing. The Open and its spread into the breadth of the unlimited and limitless is rather the zone in which supports are lacking and in which every dwelling is lost in the untenable. The Open grants no sheltering and no safety. The Open is rather the playspace of what is still indefinite and undecided and therefore the opportunity for erring and error. Thus two things remain questionable with regard to the Open: on the one hand, that and how it, originating from incipient freedom, should be the incipient essence of unconcealment; on the other hand, how the Open can be possessed of a sheltering essence.[8]

We must be careful to note that only the first two sentences in this passage embody Heidegger's own view. The Open or the free is the sheltering of being. After further inquiry into what Heidegger's Open is *not,* what the supposedly common view of the Open is, we want to pursue the central question beginning to emerge here: How can the Open shelter and keep safe?

But first we must take a look at what the bulk of this passage is describing: what the Open is *not*. It is very close to Heidegger's description of Rilke's Open. This passage can help us to round out our understanding of what it is about the Open that Heidegger absolutely and emphatically wants to distance from his own conception.

What is most striking about the common conception of the Open, should there be such a thing, is that it has no limits or boundaries of any possible sort. As such, it is utterly unable to shelter, support, or uphold anything. On reading the description of this Open, one gets the feeling of reeling about in weightless dizziness, unable to move coherently and directly or to come to rest.

The Open as Heidegger conceives it is to be thought, not as what is incapable of limits, but as cleared, illumined space that keeps safe. The Open is not just empty space; it is 'enlightened' space that shelters. Whereas in later writings Heidegger will play down the intrinsic intimacy between the Opening and light, in this lecture course he is still emphasizing that intimacy. The reason for this may lie partly in his wish to give a qualitative determination to the Open, as opposed to the sheerly spatial determination as lacking all limits.

Putting this in Heidegger's own language, the difficulty with the Open is that it is not a metaphysical concept. Metaphysical thinking proceeds by starting with the physical, sensuous, and concrete and moving on to the metaphysical, supersensuous, and abstract. With regard to the Open as a metaphysical concept, this would mean thinking of some sort of extended space and then thinking everything 'in' that extended space out of and away from it. This is comparable to what Kant did for space and time as pure forms of sensibility. Space and time are the framework in which we perceive anything at all. We can 'think away' all things, but not the framework within which we perceive things. Pure space and pure time are the structure of our minds. They alone remain after we have thought everything away.

But, according to Heidegger, this kind of thinking will never lead us to what he means by the Open. Spoken in his earlier language, we can never get to being by representing beings. We have to start with beings; they are what surrounds us. But instead of being preoccupied with *what* beings are, we might try to encounter the naked 'it is'. This would not mean asking ourselves the question whether or not something factually exists, but simply being struck by Pure 'isness'. It would mean the shift from asking Leibniz's, Schelling's, and Heidegger's question, Why is there something rather than nothing? to simply being astounded that anything is at all. Leibniz answered this question; for Schelling the answer is no longer so important; for Heidegger an answer misses the point.

> But the Open in the sense of the essence of *aletheia* means neither space nor time in the usual sense nor their unity timespace, because all of these borrow their openness from that Open that reigns in the essence of revealing. In the same way, everywhere where something is 'free' from . . . in the sense of 'empty' or 'free' 'for' in the sense of ready for . . . ,something free presences which presences out of that freeing that first sets free time-space to be traversed as the 'open' extension and expansion. The 'free from' and the 'free for' already need an Opening in which a disengaging or inclination are what they are, thus a more primordial freeing that cannot be grounded in the freedom of human behavior. We never get to the Open as the essence of *aletheia* by broadening what is familiar to us as the 'free' step by step continuously, so to speak, into an enormous container that 'embraces' everything. Strictly speaking, the essence of the Open reveals itself only to the thinking that attempts to think being itself.[9]

Metaphysical thinking thinks beings in terms of their being grounded and caused by other beings, ultimately tracing everything back to a highest being and cause of itself. By contrast, Heidegger wants to take the leap of thinking, not of faith, into the 'it is', the 'isness' of beings. If being is not to be thought as some kind of being and not as nothing at all, then it must be thought as a dimension of beings inaccessible to metaphysical thinking. This is why Heidegger relinquished the conception of being as *das transcendens schlechthin,* absolute transcendence. But this does not mean that being is simply immanent. The traditional concepts of transcendence and immanence are incapable of expressing what Heidegger is trying to get at.

> Everywhere and always and in the closest proximity of the most inconspicuous beings the Open of the possibility presences of explicitly thinking that "it is" of beings and the free in whose Opening unconcealed beings *appear*. The Open, into which every being is freed as into its free element (*sein Freies*), *the Open is being itself.* Everything unconcealed is as such sheltered in the Open of being, i.e., in the ground-less.[10]

We now tentatively begin to explore Heidegger's conception of *die Lichtung,* the Opening or clearing, as the presupposition of *both* concealment and unconcealment. I should like to underscore the fact that whenever Heidegger talked about this term, it was very clear that it had a certain magic for him. He was also concerned that it not be confused with Rilke's conception of the Open, which may, in part, be the reason why *die Lichtung* gradually came to be preferred over *das Offene.* Both words point to the Same. But for him *die Lichtung* had a special power of *naming,* which nearly puts it on par with *das Ereignis* as a later name for being.

Gradually, Heidegger comes to distance the meaning of 'light' from *die Lichtung.* In German, *Licht* means 'light', as anyone comparing the two terms can see. Accordingly, many translators have rendered the term in English as 'lighting'. From the following passages to be quoted, we can see that this is not without problems.

> Only by virtue of light, i.e., through brightness, can what shines show itself, that is, radiate. But brightness in its turn rests upon something open, something free which it might illuminate here and there, now and then. Brightness plays in the open and wars there with darkness.[11]

The war between brightness and darkness, that is, between unconcealing and concealing, takes place within the Open. The Open is prior to lightness and darkness. It does not *cause* them nor, for that matter, anything else; but it must be 'there' for anything to be able to occur.

> We call this openness which grants a possible letting-appear and show 'opening.' In the history of language, the German word is a borrowed translation of the French *clairière.* It is formed in accordance with the older words *Waldung* (foresting) and *Feldung* (fielding).
> The forest clearing (opening) is experienced in contrast to dense forest, called density (*Dickung*) in older language. The substantive 'opening' goes back to the verb 'to open' (*lichten*). The adjective *licht* 'open' is the same word as 'light' (*leicht*). To open something means: to make something light, free and open, e.g., to make the forest free of trees at one place. The openness thus originating is the clearing. What is light in the sense of being free and open has nothing in common with the adjective 'light,' meaning 'bright'—neither linguistically nor factually. This is to be observed for the difference between

openness and light. Still, it is possible that a factual relation between the two exists. Light can stream into the clearing, into its openness, and let brightness play with darkness in it. But light never first creates openness. Rather, light presupposes openness. However, the clearing, the opening, is not only free for brightness and darkness, but also for resonance and echo, for sounding and diminishing sound. The clearing is the open for everything that is present and absent.[12]

Here the dimension of hearing and sound, always important for Heidegger, contributes to our understanding of the Opening. Not only is the Opening necessary for light to appear so that we may see, but also for sound to resonate that we may hear.

> We must think *aletheia*, unconcealment, as the opening which first grants Being and thinking and their presencing to and for each other. The quiet heart of the opening is the place of stillness from which alone the possibility of the belonging together of Being and thinking, can arise at all.[13]

In this passage, the Opening is even the presupposition for *Ereignis*, Appropriation, for the belonging together of man and being. But it is not important to say what is the presupposition for what here. As Nietzsche said, he liked to sit on different rungs of his ladder. This means that Heidegger comes to different names for what he initially called "being", according to the context in which he finds himself. The Opening, Appropriation, and the Fourfold are all ultimate names for being; none needs to ground or even be the presupposition for the other. The whole business of grounding and presuppositions is still a hangover from metaphysical thinking.

> There is presence only when opening is dominant. Opening is named with *aletheia*, unconcealment, but not thought as such.[14]

The creative tension between poet and thinker is at play here. Whereas Heidegger often intimates that the poet's *naming* is something more direct and special than the thinker's *saying*, naming in this case appears to fall short of what thinking might accomplish.

After some more reflection on the Opening, we shall turn to Appropriation and to the question of its relation to Framing. This will involve a discussion of concealment as process, which we have already touched upon, and concealment as structure. Finally, we shall consider the Fourfold, eventually coming to this question: Is there concealment in the Fourfold? All of this is not yet quite as clearly organized as it might be. We are asking some questions that Heidegger does not ask so that there is no order prefigured or prescribed in his writings. On the other hand, we do not wish to superimpose a rigid order from the outside on his thought.

Appropriation   9

We are now finally ready to move the question of concealment and unconcealment to its larger, proper context. We must ask what concealment and unconcealment have to do with the later, most mature exposition of Framing and Appropriation. Since we have already discussed Framing to some extent in the context of concealment as distortion, we shall now attempt to throw some light on Appropriation, starting with what Heidegger says about the *relation* of these two.

> Thus man necessarily belongs to-, and has his place in, the openness (and at present in the forgottenness) of Being. But in order to open itself, being needs man as the there of its revealedness (*Offenbarkeit*).[1]

Man belongs to the *openness* of being. But at present he dwells in the *forgottenness* of being. "At present" does not just mean right now, perhaps in the twentieth century, but rather throughout the history of Western philosophy as metaphysics. However, since metaphysics has a history, it goes somewhere; it has led us to the completion of metaphysics as technology, the present epoch of being. This period, says Heidegger, is particularly "critical," both in the usual sense of that word as 'dangerous' and in its more precise sense as 'decisive' (from *krinein*). It was in this precise sense that Kant used the term *Kritik* for his three main works. A *Kritik* separates what can be known from what cannot.

We now dwell more in the forgottenness (*lethe*) than in the openness (*aletheia*) of being. Only the experience of Appropriation is going to be able to get us to being itself, as opposed to the ordering and production of beings in which we are now engaged. Appropriation is the belonging together of man and being where man stands within and perdures the Opening of being.

An excellent way to approach the Appropriation would be to look into the essence of Framing, since it is a passageway from metaphysics to the other kind of thinking [called a "Janus head" in *On Time and Being*, p. 53], for Framing is essentially ambiguous. "The Principle of Identity" already said: Framing (the gathering unity of all ways of placing) is the completion and fulfillment of metaphysics and at the same time the revealing preparations of Appropriation. For this reason it is not a question of viewing the rise of technology as a negative occurrence (but not as a positive occurrence in the sense of a paradise on earth either). Framing is, so to speak, the photographic negative of Appropriation.[2]

The somewhat inscrutable relation of Framing and Appropriation is captured in this passage. Framing is the completion of metaphysics and *at the same time* prepares for and reveals Appropriation. Framing is a Janus head with two faces looking in opposite directions. In some way difficult to understand or spell out, Framing and Appropriation are present at the same time. The image of the photographic negative, which is suggestive but hardly more than that, involves the simultaneity of Framing and Appropriation.

However, in *Identity and Difference*, Appropriation is envisioned as something not yet arrived—indeed, as something which may not come about at all.

No one can know whether and when and where and how this step back of thinking will develop into a proper (needed in appropriation) path and way and road-building. Instead, the rule of metaphysics may rather entrench itself, in the shape of modern technology with its developments rushing around boundlessly. Or, everything that results by way of the step back may merely be exploited and absorbed by metaphysics in its own way, as the result of representational thinking. Thus the step back would itself remain unaccomplished, and the path which it opens and points out would remain untrod.[3]

The key issue here lies with representational thinking. Representational and calculative thinking and the whole technological stance of production and ordering all perpetrate the activity of Framing. The basic characteristic of this activity is that it lets nothing be what it 'is'; it manipulates everything. The task of thinking at the end of philosophy, at the end of metaphysics, lies in relinquishing representational, calculative, and manipulative thinking in favor of letting things be and perceiving them as they are. This, of course, is a very important topic which we just mention here.

With the term 'Appropriation', Heidegger is attempting to think something probably unprecedented and perhaps not totally feasible. It is a question of how far back he can bend language. He now wants to think being itself without regard to its relation to beings as their ground. But he in no way wants to think being without regard to its relation to man. On the contrary, being is not thinkable without regard to its relation to man. This is not meant only in the Kantian sense that we can only perceive being as it appears to us, never as it is in itself. Being *needs* man in order to open itself, man as the place, the 'there', of being's arrival.

> Thus man necessarily belongs and has his place in the openness (and at present in the forgottenness) of being. But being needs man as the there of its openness in order to open itself. . . . If being needs man in this way in order to be, a *finitude of being* must be assumed accordingly. The fact that being is not absolutely for itself is the extreme opposite of Hegel. For when Hegel says that the Absolute is not "without us," he says it only with regard to the Christian "God needs men." In contrast, for Heidegger's thinking being is not without its relation to *Dasein*.[4]

In addition to finitude as concealment—more precisely, as distortion and eventually as technology—Heidegger here states that the finitude of being lies in its need for the human being. An additional dimension of finitude lies in the groundlessness of being, a dimension anticipated by Schelling. These meanings of finitude are not mutually exclusive or contradictory, but their relation has yet to become clear.

Not only does being need man; the relation between man and being is more fundamental than either man or being. The relation first determines its "components." This presents considerable difficulties for our traditional way of thinking. We cannot substantialize or objectify either man or being.

Heidegger attempts to clarify this in *Identity and Difference* with the help of one of his favorite devices: a change of emphasis in intonation. Taking Appropriation as belonging together, if the emphasis is on the *together,* we are thinking metaphysically.

> If we think of belonging *together* in the customary way, the meaning of belonging is determined by the word *together,* that

is, by its unity. In that case, 'to belong' means as much as: to be
assigned and placed into the order of a 'together,' established
in the unity of a manifold, combined into the unity of a system,
mediated by the unifying center of an authoritative synthesis.
Philosophy represents this belonging together as *nexus* and
connexio, the necessary connection of the one with the other.[5]

The customary, traditional way of thinking a relation between
two things is to first take each thing by itself and then think how
they are related and connected within the framework of a together.
This procedure corresponds to the metaphysical demands of system-
atic thinking, epitomized by the German Idealists.

When we understand thinking to be the distinctive characteristic of man, we remind ourselves of a *belonging* together that
concerns man and Being. . . . How would it be if, instead of te-
naciously representing merely a coordination of the two in order to produce the unity, we were for once to note whether and
how a belonging to one another first of all is at stake in this
'together'. . . . But man's distinctive feature lies in this, that
he, as the being who thinks, is open to Being, face to face with
Being; thus man remains referred to Being and so answers to
it. Man is essentially this relationship of responding to Being,
and he is only this.[6]

The responding of the '*belonging* together' of man and being is
contrasted with the manipulating of 'belonging *together*'. The manipulating and ordering that challenged nature to deliver energy
that can be stored for eventual use is characteristic of belonging *together,* of Framing. All of this challenging and manipulating activity
is the diametric opposite of letting be. It lets nothing be but demands of everything, humans included, that it supply material and
energy to be stored up. A response in this situation is impossible because nothing is permitted to be what it is so that we could respond
to it. Response is nothing passive or reactive; it is the essential human deed. People with severe depression are in what is perhaps the
most unbearable state there is, because they are utterly unable to
respond to anything at all. Even pain or suffering can be preferable
to that since they are, after all, some sort of response. Without some
kind of response, no poet would write a poem, no composer would
write a symphony, nobody would fall in love, no one would find a
friend. We need to ponder more deeply what it means to respond.

But we are not yet, at present, in a position to respond to being.

What we experience in the frame as the constellation of Being and man through the modern world of technology is a prelude to what is called the event of appropriation. This event, however, does not necessarily persist in its prelude. For in the event of appropriation the possibility arises that it may overcome the mere dominance of the frame to turn it into a more original appropriating. Such a transformation of the frame into the event of appropriation, by virtue of that event, would bring the appropriate recovery—appropriate, hence never to be produced by man alone—of the world of technology from its dominance back to servitude in the realm by which man reaches more truly into the event of appropriation.[7]

In this passage, Framing is not exactly conceived as coexistent with Appropriation, but as its prelude. From what Heidegger writes about the situation of his time and the world wars, and from what we can observe of our own time, we would have to say that what we are experiencing is hardly determined by Appropriation, but dominated by Framing. But, as Heidegger repeatedly emphasizes, Appropriation or being is not off somewhere waiting in the wings for the proper time to appear. Any sort of 'off-stage' belongs to the dream of metaphysics which has turned into a nightmare. The forgottenness and abandonment of being, both terms encompassing a subjective and an objective genitive, do not mean that being is somewhere off by itself, apart from our world. Where could that be? In rejecting all kinds of traditional transcendence, Heidegger has not become some brand of empiricist. Being or Appropriation is right here, but is unable to presence in an appropriate way, in the manner of Appropriation. Since all that we reckon with and take into account are beings, being is forgotten and abandoned. Ultimately, it may be that being forgets and abandons us. But, as Heidegger repeatedly stresses, being *needs* human being. Everything has been flattened down to a level where there are only beings. We do not even experience an *absence* of being; we do not even see the possibility of such a dimension. The *difference* between being and beings, between world and thing, has been forgotten and therefore the identity, or belonging together, of being and man. The difference is no longer to be conceived as an ontological one, and identity is no longer to be conceived as a flat equation between two things.

The dif-ference is not abstracted from world and thing as their relationship after the fact. The dif-ference for world and thing *disclosingly appropriates* things into bearing a world; it *disclosingly appropriates* world into the granting of things. The dif-ference is neither distinction nor relation. The dif-ference is, at most, dimension for world and thing. But in this case 'dimension' also no longer means a precinct already present independently in which this or that comes to settle. The dif-ference is *the* dimension, insofar as it measures out, apportions, world and thing, each to its own.[8]

This is strongly reminiscent of Heidegger's characterization of the Greek *moira*, fate. The term 'dimension' takes on a more and more decisive cast in Heidegger's later thought. In some ways it is preferable to the term 'dif-ference', since 'dimension' connotes a stretching out of expanse which lacks the limits of two things between which there is such an expanse. It is almost impossible for us to think difference other than as something lying between two things. Dimension dispenses with the things. Nevertheless, difference, identity, and dimension all name the same matter.

We now try to distance ourselves somewhat from Heidegger's texts and state the question of this study as clearly as possible. This question is not a matter of value judgments based upon some misguided subjectivity, but it is a matter of soteriology. It is hardly a matter of chance that Heidegger speaks more and more of the danger and the saving power growing within it. There is an undeniably menacing aspect to the danger and to Framing as the essence of technology. These cannot be identical with concealment thought as preservation and harboring. There has to be some differentiation here. Is forgottenness something that ineluctably belongs to being? If it is, then why does Heidegger speak of awakening to Appropriation? Viewed from another angle, it is highly unlikely that Heidegger envisions Framing and Appropriation as ultimately coexistent. Either we get stuck in Framing or some sort of breakthrough to Appropriation comes about. Heidegger has definitely stated that we do not know which of these two possibilities are in store for us. But, ultimately, one or the other must prevail.

What Heidegger rejects is quite clear: metaphysics. Metaphysics is *not* the sheltering, preserving, and harboring of being, but rather its perversion. There is no possible belonging together of man and being in the situation of Framing. Framing absolutely blocks any possible letting be. As long as Framing prevails as manipulating, calculating, and ordering, nothing can be what it is.

This either-or of Framing and Appropriation is expressed in Heidegger's frequent use of a change of intonation in statements to indicate a radical shift of meaning. For example, in the lecture course *The Principle of Ground*, Heidegger shows that there are two possible ways of hearing the statement, "Nothing is without a ground."

Nothing is *without* a ground.

Nothing *is* without a *ground*.

The statement heard in the first intonation is a metaphysical one: Being withdraws and conceals itself in favor of letting the ground appear as principle and cause. The statement heard in the second intonation is thought, not metaphysically, but in terms of the history of being: Being grounds in the sense of letting lie before, and itself has no ground, itself is groundless.

The question of ground is by no mean restricted to *The Principle of Ground*. In addition to "On the Essence of Ground," there is a considerable amount written on ground in the Beiträge (*Contributions*). There Heidegger distinguishes between ground, primal ground (*Urgrund*), abyss (*Abgrund*), and unground (*Ungrund*). Three of these differentiations are a matter of highly subtle differences, not oppositions or even contrasts. Primal ground is simply the deeper dimension of ground. The abyss is the 'activity' of the ground, the unity of its timing or temporalizing and spacing (*Zeit-Raum*) which includes the element of its absence. The only real oppositional factor is the unground.

The first and most important question is, What does Heidegger mean by ground? He does not mean a *cause* in any of the Aristotelian senses of that word. Here we should recall his constant polemic against the concept of God as cause of itself (*causa sui*).

> And what is the ground? It is what veils itself—what receives because it supports. It bears by towering through what is to be grounded: self-concealing in the towering through that supports.[1]

Heidegger's treatment of the ground can throw some light on our question of concealment as preservation or as distortion. In an earlier passage from the same work he gives the following short diagram:

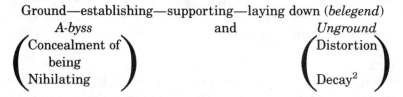

'Ground' is the basic term; its function is to support, to provide a firm basis. The a-byss[3] is the acting, 'negative' side of the ground. Just as in "What is Metaphysics?" we are told that the nothing is the veil of being, the negativity, the negating function of the ground is emphasized here. That is what prevents us from representing it as some kind of substantial thing, object, or being. The unground clearly presents the dimension of errancy and distortion. We see here an analysis roughly parallel to that of concealment.

> Truth: ground as abyss. Ground not from where, but wherein as what belongs. *Abgrund* as the time-space of the strife.[4]

Ground is not that *out of which* something *proceeds,* but *wherein* something *belongs.* Any idea of efficient causality as making and producing is totally out of place here. The ground in no sense precedes that for which it is the ground; it is a *priori* neither in a temporal nor a logical sense. The ground is not a condition of possibility either. The basically Kantian position of much of *Being and Time* has been relinquished; and yet Heidegger still retains the word 'ground'.

The question then becomes, Ground *for what?* The highly paradoxical answer, gleaned from many intriguing, and at times almost maddening, attempts to state what is to be said, must finally read: ground for the abyss. What is the abyss? The time-space of *Da-sein,* what Heidegger in *Beiträge* frequently calls "the place of the moment" (*Augenblicksstätte*). The abyss is the time-space where something essential and crucial can occur. It could be the time-space for the flight and arrival of the gods; it could be the time-space and opportunity for the other beginning.

This is not the place to go into a detailed analysis of what Heidegger means by time-space. Suffice it to say that he does not, of course, have in mind the traditional concepts of time or space. The abyss is a kind of emptiness (*Leere*), but not the empty space for things or the empty time for events. Time and space conceived in this basically Newtonian, later Kantian, way are pictured as containers, as that *in which* things and events occur. Heidegger has always attempted to think a nonspatial 'in'. When I am *in* a good mood, I am not in a container.

> The a-byss as the ground's remaining absent in the sense mentioned is the first opening of the open as 'emptiness.'
>
> But which emptiness is intended here? Not the unoccupied one of the ordering forms and frameworks for calculable and objectively present space and time, not the absence of things objectively present within these, but the temporal-spatial emptiness, the original gaping in hesitating self-refusal.
>
> The openness of the clearing of concealment is thus originally not the mere emptiness of being unoccupied, but rather the attuned and attuning emptiness of the a-byss.[5]

There is no real opposition between ground and abyss. Mostly Heidegger formulates the relation between them by saying that the abyss is the working or functioning of the ground. The ground functions by remaining absent (*Weg-bleiben*), thus allowing emptiness to originate. All of these terms—'emptiness' (*die Leere*), 'the open' (*das Offene*), and 'the clearing' (*die Lichtung*)—attempt to name something absolutely nonsubstantial. This is always difficult, if not bordering on the impossible. It explains the constant self-contradictions in most of Heidegger's formulations. No sooner does he have a term, a noun, than he immediately adds an adjective that contradicts the ordinary meaning of that term. Heidegger makes such extensive use of this device that it seems superfluous to give examples.

> A-byss is remaining absent; as the ground in self-concealment, a self-concealment in the manner of the refusal of the ground. However, refusal is not nothing, but rather a distinctive original way of leaving unfilled and empty; thus a distinctive way of opening. But as the presencing of the ground the a-byss is not merely self-refusal as a simple retreat and withdrawal. The *a*-byss is a-*byss*. In self-refusal the ground brings into the open in a distinctive way, namely in the first open of *that* emptiness which is thus a definite one. Since the ground grounds also and precisely in the abyss and yet does not really ground, it hesitates.[6]

One is tempted to try to fit all of this into the familiar Heideggerian schema of man and being. Accordingly, being or primal being would be the ground and man would be the *abyss,* the 'place' where being can come to presence. But this will not quite do. In the thinking of the Appropriation (*Ereignis*), the clear-cut distinction between man and being no longer exists. What we have is the *relation* between man and being as what is more primordial than both and first allows man and being to originate. Thus, we cannot just say that being is the ground and man is the abyss. It is not the case that there is no distinction at all between man and being; they do not just coalesce in an unarticulated identity. That would be the proverbial night in which all cows are black. And we know from *Identity and Difference* that Heidegger thinks identity as belonging together.

> But this nearest self-concealment is only the appearance of the a-byss and thus of the truth of Appropriation. But the truth presences in the most complete and pure clearing of

the farthest self-concealing only in the manner of sheltering
(*Bergung*). . . . Sheltering moves self-concealing into the open
just as sheltering itself is ruled by the *clearing* of self-
concealment.[7]

This passage focuses on two elements: sheltering and the
clearing of self-concealment. It is not sufficient to have the clearing
of self-concealment as one might expect; this clearing of self-
concealment must itself be sheltered. In other passages from the
same context (*Beiträge*), however, it seems that what is to be sheltered is not the clearing of self-concealment, but self-concealment
itself.

From where does sheltering have its need and necessity? From
self-concealing. In order not to remove self-concealing, rather
to preserve it, the sheltering of this *occurrence* is needed. . . .
The sheltering of self-concealing must always be.[8]

One might think that self-concealing would be, so to speak, automatically sheltering at the same time. After all, what conceals
itself is not exposed. We saw earlier that one of the possible meanings of concealment was precisely preserving. Perhaps the most
that can be said at this point is that the element of self-concealing
seems to be absolutely fundamental, certainly at least in the history of being as metaphysics. The question then becomes whether
self-concealment or something similar also has a place in Appropriation. We shall come back to this.

Returning to the question of ground, another text can throw
some light on the problem. As stated before, ground and abyss are
not opposites. Nor are they identical (*das Gleiche*); they are the
Same (*das Selbe*). What does this mean?

Being 'is' in essence: ground. For this reason being can never
have a ground that is supposed to ground it. Accordingly, the
ground remains absent from being. In the sense of the ground's
remaining absent (*Ab-bleibens*) from being, being 'is' the a-byss
(*Ab-Grund*). Since being as such is of a grounding nature
(*gründend ist*), it itself remains without a ground.[9]

In the context of this lecture course, we learn that being is the
ground insofar as it provides the basis for beings. As previously
mentioned, ground and basis by no means coincide with efficient
cause. Being does not cause or produce beings. It is simply that upon

which beings stand, lie, or rest. Heidegger's thought is quite close to that of Schelling in the treatise on human freedom here. The concepts of unground, abyss, and withdrawal also owe much to Schelling. Heidegger did, after all, devote a whole lecture course to that treatise.

But as the ground for beings, being itself has no ground. This does not mean that it is the traditionally thought cause of itself, *causa sui*. The cause of itself, God, is still *a being*. Heidegger's being can in no sense of the word be a being. The later names for being bear witness to this. Appropriation (*Ereignis*) names a relation, not a being. The Fourfold (*das Geviert*) again names an even more complex relation. And the clearing (*die Lichtung*) designates a kind of empty place in which beings can presence.

Being is the a-byss. It is ground and abyss at the same time. It provides the ground for beings, but it itself has no ground and is thus abyss.

Having tried to think about what 'ground' means, we can return to the shift in intonation in the proposition: nothing is without ground. Heard in the manner of the second intonation, the statement sounds as follows: Nothing *is* without a *ground*. The statement emphasizes that belonging together of being and ground. The other kind of intonation, *Nothing* is *without* a ground, is a metaphysical one. It characterizes the first beginning (of the history of Being) as the history of forgottenness of being. That is the history of Western metaphysics. That history included the long incubation of the principle of ground. This incubation period came to an end with Leibniz, who proclaimed the principle of ground as the highest principle. It is always astounding to see the excitement and enthusiasm with which Leibniz discussed the principle of ground. Everyone had known for a long, long time that all things have a cause. But Leibniz seemed to think he had discovered something new in that principle, and in a certain sense he had. With Leibniz the principle first gained its status as the highest principle.

> When the incubation of the principle of ground comes to an end with the positing of the principle of ground as a highest principle, the end of this incubation must lie in the fact that meanwhile the destiny of being has turned, supposedly in the sense that being as such has awakened and brings itself to appearance. *But this is precisely not what happens at the end of the incubation period of the principle of ground.* Something has indeed turned in the destiny of being, but in a completely different sense. In that the principle of ground expressly gains

dominance as the highest principle, the true power of the principle of ground as *principium rationis* is first set loose.[10]

With the end of its incubation period, the principle of ground has explicitly become the principle of *reason* with its demand to find a cause for everything. The result is that being withdraws itself even more decisively. Beings have become objects for representational thinking; being sends itself as the objectivity of objects (*die Gegenständigkeit der Gegenstände*).

Heidegger deals with this situation in various ways and contexts in almost all of his writings. We want to look into what he is more reticent to speak about: the possibility of the other beginning (*der andere Anfang*), of a belonging together of man and being, Appropriation, and the Fourfold. Our question is not clearly and totally answerable as long as we remain strictly with what Heidegger actually said. Ultimately we shall attempt some tentative speculation of our own, speculation yet firmly rooted in Heidegger's thought. That question is, What, if any, is the place of concealment and withdrawal in Appropriation? In the Fourfold?

A further question resulting from that one is, What does it mean if there is no concealment and withdrawal? What would that 'look like'? And if concealment and/or withdrawal do belong ineluctably to being, what does *that* mean?

Part of the reason that concealment is so important to Heidegger is that it prevents us from considering being as a being. It also prevents us from thinking of being as infinite. Here Heidegger remains true to his roots in Greece. To be is to be something that has limit (*peras*). As Nietzsche pointed out, the Greeks had a horror of infinity. They thought of infinity as nothingness. The Judeo-Christian emphasis on infinity as a necessary, positive attribute of God was completely foreign to the Greeks. But it certainly has had a profound influence on almost all of our philosophers ever since.

The ground is not a cause; the abyss is not simply an infinite, empty nothingness.

The Open of the abyss is not groundless. Abyss is not the no to every ground as is groundlessness, but the yes to the ground in its concealed expanse and distance. . . . The a-byss is as little 'negative' as the hesitating denial (*Versagung*); both, immediately (logically) intended, contain a 'no,' and yet the hesitating denial is the first and highest gleam of the beckoning (*der Wink*).[11]

To conclude this discussion of ground and abyss, ground is to be sharply differentiated from cause, and abyss is not to be confused with a kind of infinite nothingness. What is opposed to both is the un-ground.

> The abyss, however, is completely distorted by the un-ground. . . . The answer lies in reflecting on the fact that the abyss, barely grounded, was already buried by the un-ground.[12]

Spoken in the context of the ground, this is another way of saying that concealment overcame unconcealment at the very beginning of the history of being.

We turn now to the extremely difficult, if not insoluble, question of the relation of concealment to Appropriation and to the Fourfold. As a kind of *via negativa* we turn briefly to what Heidegger has to say about nihilism and the history of being.[13] Nihilism, metaphysics, and ontotheology are all names for the same thing: the history of being in which being remains unthought, thus actually the history of the abandonment and forgottenness of being. Metaphysics and ontotheology claim to think being, but they translate it into a being, the highest being, the cause of itself, or some sort of *a priori*. Being itself remains absent. This is the meaning of nihilism. *Nothing* happens with being itself. (*"Das Wesen des Nihilismus ist die Geschichte, in der es mit dem Sein nichts ist"*). This does not mean that being is somewhere else than in the history of being as nihilism. There is nowhere else for being to be. And being is not *a* being that could be somewhere else. Being is unlocalizable; it cannot be pin-pointed anywhere in space and time as they are ordinarily conceived. This is the enormous difficulty. Up to now, all that our thinking has been able to do is to think *beings*. We are told that this is not due to some oversight or deficiency in our thinking. Being has simply remained absent. Being is not anywhere else; it presences *as this remaining absent.*

> Being itself presences as the unconcealment in which beings come to presence. Unconcealment itself, however, remains concealed as such. With reference to itself, unconcealment as such remains absent. *The matter stands with the concealment of the presencing of unconcealment. It stands with the concealment of being as such. Being itself remains absent.*[14]

How are we to think the presencing of being as remaining absent? Remaining absent is by no means simply nothing. Without being, beings could not "be" at all. What presences is the *concealment* of being. Concealment is not nothing; nor is it something.

> Rather, in remaining absent, there presences a relation to something like place, away from which remaining absent remains what it is; the remaining absent of unconcealment as such. That place is the shelter in which the remaining absent of unconcealment essentially persists. However, if concealment persists in the remaining absent of unconcealment as such, then the remaining of concealment also retains its essential relation to that same place.[15]

Heidegger is trying to steer between the Scylla and Charybdis of nugatory nothingness (*das nichtige Nichts*) and the objective presence (*Vorhandenheit*) of a being. His whole philosophical enterprise is the attempt to think the presencing of being other than as objective presence which can always be only that of a being. All of his later "metaphors" for being do not name a being, but a relation (Appropriation and the Fourfold) or, at best, some kind of cleared, empty place (*Lichtung*).

Unconcealment remains absent; concealment remains. Both of these statements affirm and deny a kind of presence at the same time. The term 'dialectic' was anathema to Heidegger from the very beginning. Still, there is a kind of Heraclitean dialectic at work (or at play) here. Heraclitus is known for the famous fragment stating that one cannot step in the same river twice. But the full formulation of that thought is to be found in the fragment which states that one does and one does not step in the same river twice.

Given these limitations of language—limitations which Heidegger is inclined to attribute to Western languages—one is tempted to say that language is the house, not of being, but of *beings*. There just may not be a language of 'being', not in Eastern languages either. Why else would the brilliant second century Indian thinker Nagarjuna have formulated his tetralemma consisting of four kinds of statements that cannot be made. One may not say:

It is.
It is not.
It both is and is not.
It neither is nor is not.

That pretty much exhausts the possibilities of predication. Many thinkers have been acutely aware of the limitations of language, the outstanding recent example being Ludwig Wittgenstein.

Some thinkers have also succeeded in pushing back those limitations to some degree.

Heidegger seems to be walking a kind of ontological tightrope in his attempt to avoid the two extremes of presence (objective presence) and absence (nugatory nothingness). These two simple extremes are all that the language of metaphysics is equipped to express. In discussing nihilism, which is where the history of being (which actually is the history of the absence of being) has led us, Heidegger goes back to two adjectival terms, prominent in *Being and Time,* with whose help he hopes to characterize nihilism as other than mere nothingness. Even, or perhaps especially, nihilism admits of differentiation. Those two terms are *'eigentlich'* and *'uneigentlich',* translated in *Being and Time* as 'authentic' and 'inauthentic', respectively. We know that these terms played a larger part in the structure of that book. The whole fabric of experience differs according to whether it is authentic or inauthentic—even the experience of time derives from authenticity or inauthenticity according to the way temporality temporalizes itself. In the later context of nihilism, *eigentlich* and *uneigentlich* are better translated as appropriate and inappropriate. Both English terms 'authentic' and 'appropriate', have the same root as the German *eigen,* self; authentic has the Greek *auto;* appropriate has the Latin *proprius.*

Heidegger speaks of appropriate and inappropriate nihilism. Appropriate nihilism lies in the fact that being remains absent (*bleibt aus*). This is simply what has happened and what is happening. We are not told why; this is not of our doing at all. Inappropriate nihilism, then, consists in the fact that this remaining absent of being is neglected, left out (*ausgelassen*). This we have something to do with, although it doesn't originate with us. We perpetrate this neglect but are not the originating source of it.

> But insofar as this remaining absent occurs in metaphysics, what is appropriate is not admitted *as* what is appropriate to nihilism. Rather, remaining absent is left out precisely in the thinking of metaphysics in such a way that metaphysics even leaves out this leaving out as its own deed.[16]

Since the subject of all this is metaphysics, the deed is removed from the sphere of human being as conceived by psychology, anthropology, etc. The question of responsibility cannot be explored here. Suffice it to say that it lies ultimately with being, which leaves us with many unanswered, perhaps unanswerable, questions.

But there is an enigmatic factor here which is more intriguing and which may derive some of its impetus from Heidegger's work with Schelling's treatise on human freedom. That factor is the primordial *unity* of appropriate and inappropriate nihilism.

The complete essence of nihilism is the primordial unity of what is appropriate and what is inappropriate in it.[17]

Inappropriate nihilism is identical with metaphysics. As long as inappropriate nihilism remains in its essential unity with appropriate nihilism, being is not completely jeopardized. It still retains some kind of shelter. When we consider that being *needs* the essence of man, the soteriological element comes to the fore here.

What is inappropriate in the essence of nihilism is the history of leaving out; that is, of the concealment of the promise. Granted, however, that being saves itself in its remaining absent, then the history of the leaving out of remaining absent is precisely the preservation of being's saving itself.[18]

The promise mentioned in this passage is being's promise. The genitive is both subjective and objective. Being does the promising (subjective), and what it promises is precisely itself (objective). Even in all this negativity, being saves itself as long as all of this occurs in the essential unity of appropriate and inappropriate nihilism. Things are still 'all right', even if they are hardly ideal.

But, Heidegger muses, the difference of the appropriate and the inappropriate ruling in the essential unity of nihilism *could*, so to speak, disrupt, splitting that essential unity.

The difference between what is inappropriate and appropriate reigning in the essential unity of nihilism could diverge into the most extreme disjunction of the inappropriate from the appropriate. In that case, in keeping with its own meaning, the essential unity of nihilism would have to conceal itself to the utmost. The essential unity would have to disappear, as though it were nothing at all, in the unconcealment of beings as such, which everywhere pass for being itself. It would then have to appear as if there were nothing to being itself, provided that such a thought could still occur at all.[19]

This is couched in the language of the subjunctive, but in what follows, Heidegger is more or less saying that if being chose to let this happen, there would be nothing man could do about it. With this discussion of inappropriate nihilism taking over, Heidegger is finally able to do justice to what can be undeniably destructive about nihilism.

> In this way, what is inappropriate in nihilism reaches uncon-ditional predominance, behind which what is appropriate, and along with what is appropriate and its relation to what is in-appropriate the essence of nihilism, remains submerged in the inaccessible and unthinkable. . . . The struggle over nihilism, for it and against it, is enacted on a field staked out by the pre-dominance of the disessence of nihilism. Nothing will be de-cided by this struggle. It will merely seal the predominance of what is inappropriate in nihilism. Even where it believes itself to be in opposition, the struggle is everywhere and at bottom nihilistic—in the usual destructive sense of that word.[20]

Once trapped in the field staked out by inappropriate nihilism, there is no possible way out within that field. The struggle for and against nihilism taking place in it is of necessity a losing battle. That battle is to be sharply distinguished from strife, the strife be-tween world and earth, which is generative and creative. That bat-tle is like Don Quixote's fight with the windmill. In Richard Strauss's tone poem of that name, throughout all the activity in the treble a bass tone remains, indicating that nothing gets off the ground; in spite of all the frenzy, nothing happens. The upshot of this is that nothing can get decided or changed *within beings.* Every attempt on the part of man to overcome nihilism is doomed from the outset. All that we can do is to think toward (*entgegendenken, an-denken*) the remaining absent of being.

When Heidegger says that we leave out leaving out the re-maining absent of being, he is not just repeating empty words. A parallel example: when I forget that I have forgotten something, whatever that is has completely vanished from the possible reach of my experience. As long as I realize that I have forgotten something, I am aware of having forgotten and will try to retrieve it. But if I forget that I have forgotten, the thing is simply gone. That is the most profound sense of forgetting.

As mentioned before, the dualities of concealment–unconcealment and inappropriate–appropriate nihilism give evidence of some influence of Schelling and also of Franz Baader and Jakob Böhme. In his *Treatise on Human Freedom,* to which Heidegger devoted an entire lecture course, Schelling differentiates between two kinds of will in the structure of all beings, including God. It is in this treatise that Schelling asserts that all primal being is will.

Schelling states that the fundamental structure, which he calls a "jointure" (*Fuge*), of every independent being is that of ground and existence. The distinction of ground and existence is rooted in the essence of primal being (i.e., will). What is the meaning of these two terms for him? Ground does not mean reason (*ratio*), but rather basis, foundation, that from which something emerges and upon which it stands. Existence does not mean factual objective presence (*Vorhandenheit*), the fact that something is there, but names the movement of emerging from itself and revealing itself. Thus, existence has to do with understanding (*lumen naturale*) and expansion, whereas ground is associated with darkness, gravity, and contraction.

The 'activity' of this structure of ground and existence, which by no means coincides with the traditional metaphysical distinction of essence and existence, then becomes a distinction of wills in accordance with the essence of all primal being as will. The ground becomes the will of the ground, self-will, the will of the particular, nonrational (not *ir*rational) longing. Existence becomes the will of the understanding and spirit, the universal will, the will of love.

The bond between these two wills, the will of the ground and the will of love, is indissoluble in God. The ground belonging to God is *within* himself, not outside of him. This is Schelling's version of the *causa sui*. He may be the only thinker who attempted to say what that expression *means* instead of just accepting it as a tradition. The ground in God is nature, that which is not God himself.

The ground is an eternal becoming, the eternal longing of the eternal One to give birth to itself.

In man, however, the bond between the will of the ground and the will of love is separable. The will of the ground, instead of remaining where it should in the function of a foundation, can assert itself in an act of insurgence and try to usurp the function of the will of love. The particular will can try to take the place of the universal will. The self-assertion of the individual will usurping the place of the universal will of love constitutes the possibility of evil.

Heidegger himself is not especially interested in the problem of evil. What, then, intrigues him about Schelling's treatise, and what influence did it have on him?

In general, what attracts Heidegger to Schelling's philosophy is its awareness of the limitation of reason and rational explanation, without therefore vaulting straight into the irrational, at which, Heidegger says in *Being and Time,* rationalism looks merely with a squint. It was Schelling's insight that not everything can be explained by reason. Ultimate things especially cannot always be explained but must be told or narrated. Thus Schelling wrote the late works *The Philosophy of Mythology* and *The Philosophy of Revelation,* which are not based on rational explanation but relate 'stories'.

Correlate with this insight is Schelling's conception of the groundless and his postulation of a dark, negative principle in all beings, including God. The postulation of a dark, negative principle continues a hermetic tendency found in Böhme and Baader.

> Thus it would require nothing less than the whole power of a deeply pondered and thoroughly developed philosophy to prove that there are only two ways of explaining evil—the dualistic, according to which there is assumed to be an evil basic being, regardless with what modifications, beneath or alongside the good; and the cabalistic, according to which evil is explained by emanation and withdrawal.[1]

Schelling himself opts for the first possibility, the assumption of an evil basic being or principle. This makes him one of the first philosophers to take evil seriously instead of branding it as a mere lack of good or as contributing to the variety and perfection of the whole, as the majority of philosophers, epitomized by the seventeenth century rationalists, had done. Yet this duality is nothing ultimate; Schelling's concept of the Absolute as the groundless and indifference is beyond all duality and antithesis.

We have already explained what we assume in the first respect: There must be a being *before* all ground and before all existence, that is, before any duality at all; how can we designate it except as 'primal ground' or, rather, as the 'groundless'? As it precedes all antitheses, these cannot be distinguishable in it or be present in any way at all. It cannot then be called the identity of both, but only the absolute indifference as to both.[2]

However, in the last analysis, Schelling pretty much espouses the traditional view of evil by saying that it is "no being, but a counterfeit of being, which is real only by contrast, not in itself."[3] With this statement, Schelling basically returns to the position of Plato, for whom evil and matter were spurious beings, something that should not be.

What is Heidegger's position in all of this? If Schelling were correct in saying that there are only two ways of explaining evil, does Heidegger fit into one of these, or is he incapable of being thus categorized? This is a question that cannot be simply answered at this point—if it can, indeed, be answered at all. The most that can be said is that he would appear to be closer to withdrawal (not, however, to emanation) as the key to evil rather than asserting a basic evil principle. Still, we are left with the question, Why is there withdrawal if there is not, after all, some dualistic tendency in being itself?

The last thing to be mentioned before returning to the question of the relation of Appropriation and concealment is the need of being, being's need.

Its [being's] remaining absent is its self-withdrawal in keeping to itself with its unconcealment which it promises in its refusing self-concealment. Thus being presences as a promise in withdrawal. But withdrawal remains a relation, the relation in which being itself lets its shelter come to it, i.e., establishes a relation to that shelter (*sie be-zieht*). As such relating, being never, even in the remaining absent of its unconcealment, lets go of that unconcealment, which in keeping to itself is released solely as the unconcealment of beings. As the arrival that never lets go of its shelter, being is the unceasing (*das Unab-lässige*). In this way it is necessitating. . . . Being needs a shelter. . . . In the arrival of the remaining absent of its unconcealment, being itself is need.[4]

"Being needs a shelter." That shelter is the essence of man, *Dasein*, the place of the moment. If man could experience the arrival of being's remaining absent, he could realize being's need for shelter. As things stand in the case of metaphysics, man is totally unaware of being's need because of his preoccupation with beings and their manipulability. The first thing he must do is not to experience being's need; that is not directly possible. First, he must experience the *lack* of need that is the most extreme form of neediness. Lack of need is the inappropriate form of nihilism, the unground. Only when he experiences the lack of need as a kind of self-sufficient, self-contained trap, a kind of superorganized inferno, can he realize that there is no place for need in this trap. For Heidegger, it is not a matter of man breaking through to an experience of transcendence; it is a matter of letting being's need *arrive here*. The traditional categories of transcendence and immanence no longer suffice for what Heidegger is attempting to think here.

We turn now to the relation of Appropriation and concealment. This will involve a consideration of concealment or its equivalent as process and as structure, a question that arises with regard to perdurance (*Austrag*) and epoch and *epochē* as well.

Heidegger states that withdrawal (*Entzug*) belongs to what is peculiar to Appropriation. He then says that a discussion of that statement no longer belongs to the matter of the lecture "Time and Being." But then he goes on to make the following remarks:

> Insofar as the destiny of being lies in the extending of time, and time, together with being, lies in Appropriation, Appropriating makes manifest its peculiar property, that Appropriation withdraws what is most fully its own from boundless unconcealment. Thought in terms of Appropriating, this means: in that sense it expropriates itself of itself. Expropriation belongs to Appropriation as such. By this expropriation, Appropriation does not abandon itself, rather, it preserves what is its own.[1]

In this particular text (*On Time and Being*) we are dealing with three names for *lethe:* withdrawal, expropriation, and concealment. This does not imply that Heidegger's different texts "contradict" themselves, but only that the particular context often requires a special focus that may not exactly coincide with other perspectives.

Appropriation, the belonging together of man and being, is not another epoch in the history of being as metaphysics. When thinking enters into Appropriation, the history of being as metaphysics comes to an end, even though metaphysics may continue on. What continues on might be compared to the long rumble of thunder that follows the lightning flash. The rumble of thunder is still there, but nothing decisive begins to happen in it. What was decisive was the lightning flash.

> Thinking then stands in and before that which has sent the various forms of epochal being. This, however, what sends as Appropriation, is itself unhistorical, or more precisely without destiny.[2]

Metaphysics has been the history of the self-withdrawal of what does the sending in favor of what is sent and allowed to presence. What sends cannot thereby send itself as well. But Heidegger goes a step further and states that not only does being not send itself; it withdraws. Withdrawing seems to be a condition of sending, or at least concomitant with it.

What has been sending is Appropriation, which itself has no history and no destiny. What has a history is what has been sent, and that is the history of metaphysics. When Heidegger talks about the history of being, he is talking about the history of the *forgottenness* of being, that is, of metaphysics.

> Metaphysics is the forgottenness of being, and that means the history of the concealment and withdrawal of that which gives being. The entry of thinking into Appropriation is thus equivalent to the end of this withdrawal's history. The forgottenness of being 'supersedes' (*hebt auf*) itself in the awakening into Appropriation.[3]

When thinking enters Appropriation, Appropriation ceases to withdraw itself. What does this mean? Heidegger is understandably reticent about this entry of thinking into Appropriation, but he has at least two things to say about it. (1) The end of the history of metaphysics as the succession of epochs of being is not the end of all activity and movement. (2) The end of the history of withdrawal is not necessarily the end of concealment as such.

re (1) The fact that Appropriation has no history does not mean that it is some kind of *stasis*. Heidegger does not deny all movement in it, but only the kind of movement that constitutes a *continuous process*. Even the history of being as metaphysics does not have the character of uninterrupted continuity. The epochs of this history of being did not follow each other organically, one growing out of the other; but were sendings from Appropriation. For example, *actualitas* (actuality) did not grow out of *energeia* (actuality), but constituted a different epoch of being, not, of course, without relation to *energeia*. The question is a tricky one. But Heidegger's epochs of being do not constitute a dialectical process like that of Hegel, where antithesis grows out of thesis and synthesis grows out of antithesis. The sendings occurred abruptly and unexpectedly without horizontal continuity.

> Thus the lack of destiny of Appropriation does not mean that it has no 'movement.' Rather, it means that the manner of movement most proper to Appropriation turning toward us in withdrawal—first shows itself as what is to be thought.[4]

The most that can be said here is probably that the movement proper to Appropriation is not one of continuous process or, for that matter, of any kind of process in the usual sense at all. The frequent reference to the place of the moment (*Augenblicks-stätte*) reinforces this lack of process.

re (2) Even though Heidegger predominantly, though not always, states that the character of withdrawal is absent from Appropriation, concealment and expropriation are still constitutive. He holds on to the element of concealment with a remarkable consistency. The question that never seems to have entered his mind is why this does not constitute a duality, if not a dualism, within being/Appropriation itself.

> But the concealment which belongs to metaphysics as its limit must belong to Appropriation itself. That means that the withdrawal which characterized metaphysics in the form of the forgottenness of being now shows itself as the dimension of concealment itself. But now this concealment does not conceal itself.[5]

What, then, is the difference between concealment and withdrawal? Withdrawal would seem to indicate a movement away from something, eventuating in increasing absence. Concealment is simply neutral. We can perhaps say that all withdrawal is a kind of concealment, but not all concealment is a kind of withdrawal. Concealment is the more comprehensive term.

This brings us back to the issue mentioned before: the question of process and structure. The term 'epoch' is especially suited to illustrate this, as is the term 'perdurance' (*Austrag*).

On the one hand, 'epoch' designates the periods of the history of being, the succession of destinies or sendings (*Schickungen*) sent or given by the 'It gives'. These epochs are not dialectically related, nor are they predictable or calculable. Thus Heidegger speaks of Plato's interpretation of being as *idea,* Aristotle's as *energeia,* Kant's as position, and so forth. These are epochs in the history of being. Epochs are here conceived as periods in some process, albeit not the traditionally conceived process of history.

On the other hand, *epochē* retains its original Greek meaning of check, holding back, keeping to itself *(Ansichhalten).* This appears to be a structure of being itself, not one of the epochs sent by being constituting the occurrence or process of history.

> The history of being means the destiny of being in whose sendings both the sending and the It which sends forth hold back with their self-manifestation. To hold back is, in Greek, *epochē.* Hence we speak of the epochs of the destiny of being. *Epochē* does not mean here a span of time in occurrence, but rather the fundamental characteristic of sending, the actual holding-back of itself in favor of the discernibility of the gift, that is, of being with regard to the grounding of beings.[6]

Here, *epochē* is a structural component of being itself. It belongs to the sending, not to what is sent. *Epochē* is another way of designating concealment, withdrawal, expropriation.

> Along the way we have already thought more about it, although it was not explicitly said: namely, that to giving as sending there belongs keeping back—such that the denial of the present and the withholding of the present, play within the giving of what has been and what will be. What we have mentioned just now—keeping back, denial, withholding—shows something like a self-withdrawing, something we might call for short: withdrawal. But inasmuch as the modes of giving that are determined by withdrawal—sending and extending— lie in Appropriation, withdrawal must belong to what is peculiar to Appropriation. This, however, no longer belongs to the matter of this lecture.[7]

What is distinctive about the expression "keeping to itself" may lie in the fact that keeping to itself is a kind of *stasis,* a lack of movement. Keeping to itself refrains from movement and activity. Here is a very ontic and very simple example that also brings out the relation between sending *(schicken)* and letting *(lassen),*

Heidegger's two terms for what being 'does': when I throw a ball, I have to *let go* of it. My hand does not go with the ball but remains behind.

Structure determines process and makes it possible. We find a similar situation with the term 'perdurance' (*Austrag*). On the one hand, Heidegger uses the term in its customary sense of carry out, bring to term (a child). Again, this designates a process with the added implication that the process is carried out to its completion. Perdurance is not ideal to translate this meaning of *Austrag*.

However, perdurance is also used in the structural sense of the Greek *diaphora*, to hold apart.

The onto-theological constitution of metaphysics stems from the prevalence of that difference which keeps being as the ground, and being as what is grounded and what gives account, apart from and related to each other; this holding apart is enacted by perdurance.

That which bears such a name directs our thinking to the realm which the key words—being and beings, the ground and what is grounded—are no longer adequate to utter. For what these words name, what the manner of thinking that is guided by them represents, originates as that which differs by virtue of the difference. The origin of the difference can no longer be thought within the scope of metaphysics.[8]

This structural sense of *Austrag* is the difference. It was named in the beginning of Western philosophy by Heraclitus.

What is opposed harmonizes and from the disharmonious arises the most beautiful harmony.

Just as Heidegger's version of identity as belonging together names a primordial relation which in some sense generates its relata, the structure of the difference first determines that which differs. Again, all of these relational terms are intended to absolutely prevent us from representing being or the difference as a being. And, as Heidegger says, this difference, or the origin of this difference, can no longer be thought in the scope of metaphysics, which, among other things, always represents being as cause.

The processual sense of *Austrag* is perhaps most richly documented in the writings on language.

The unitary fourfold sky and earth, mortals and divinities, which is stayed in the thinging of things, we call—the world.

In the naming, the things named are called into their thinging, Thinging, they unfold world, in which things abide and so
are the abiding ones. By thinging, things carry out world. Our
old language calls such carrying—*bern, baren*—Old High German, *beran*—to hear; hence the words *gebären,* to carry, *gestate,* give birth and *Gebärde,* bearing gesture. Thinging, things
are things. Thinging, they gesture—*gestate*—world.[9]

Yet if we tried to say what kind of bearing and gesturing (*gebären, Gebärde*) this is, our customary ideas about process fall
short. Western philosophy has distinguished and developed two basic conceptions of process: mechanism and teleology. Neither is appropriate to designate what Heidegger has in mind as process. A
third alternative, found only in a few thinkers, most notably Heraclitus and Nietzsche, is more appropriate. That alternative is play.
We shall return to this later.

This leaves us with alternative possibilities with regard to
both *epochē* and *Austrag.* They can be either an essential structural
component of being itself or a consequence of the history of being
(i.e., the history of the abandonment and forgottenness of being).
But the history of the abandonment of being is, after all, the history
of the abandonment of *being.* This history of being (process) ought to
have something to do with being itself (structure). The same situation should then apply, in some way, to the question of concealment.

We can see that the source of our difficulty is one that
Heidegger has already pointed out. The difficulty lies in language,
most prominently in Western language. Thus, both terms we are
trying to work with, structure and process, are themselves still
mired in metaphysical thinking. Yet if we just relinquish them altogether, we will completely lose our whole orientation. Therefore,
we shall retain them, trying to purify them as much as possible of
their metaphysical connotations. Even when these terms are "deconstructed," there remains a profound ambiguity here.

Process, in the broadest possible sense of the word, simply
means that something is going on. Given Heidegger's emphasis on
temporality from the very beginning, he is certainly speaking about
some kind of happening. All of the numerous discussions of history
and destiny (*Geschick*) bear witness to this. However, this happening is neither mechanistic nor teleological; it is not even causal. We
shall try to discuss further this kind of happening in the context of
the Fourfold.

Structure, in its broadest possible sense, means that there is
some sort of order, but we must not, as we inevitably do, think of
this order as itself something existent, as a being.

Ultimately, Heidegger may be trying to think occurrence in a way that includes something like structure. This would mean that he is trying to think structure and process as some kind of unity. This could explain why terms such as *'Austrag'* and *'epoch'* sometimes appear to tend more in the direction of a process, sometimes more in the direction of a structure. Language forces Heidegger to express himself at times more in terms of structure, at others more in terms of process. We have only nouns and verbs; we do not have noun-verbs, unless we count gerunds, which he does make use of whenever possible. But they alone will not solve the problem.

Structure corresponds roughly to space or place; process corresponds to time. We know that, from the very beginning, Heidegger has attempted to think space and time in a more primordial way. His early efforts were devoted almost exclusively to time. These efforts even went so far as to derive spatiality from temporality, a position he later retracted in the lecture "Time and Being." The later essays reinstated spatiality in its own right, and an emphasis on place and topology (*Erörterung*) gained increasing importance.

According to Heidegger, representational, calculative thinking has wreaked havoc with the concepts of space and time that, in fact, should not be conceptualized at all. Conceptualization is part of the problem inherent in representational, calculative thinking, which objectifies and reifies everything. Space is not Newtonian container space and time is not an Aristotelian string of now-points. Whereas space and time have hitherto been discussed largely in terms of measurement (how far, how long), what can be measured in space and time belongs to the most derivative element about them. If they are to be conceived as dimensions, Heidegger takes that word in its most primordial sense as a kind of measuring through that first constitutes what is to be measured. Nothing is objectively present and 'there' to begin with that could then subsequently be calculated.

The upward glance spans the between of heaven and earth. This between is measured out for the dwelling of man. We call the span (*Durchmessung*) thus meted out the dimension. This dimension does not arise from the fact that sky and earth are turned toward one another. Rather, their facing each other depends on the dimension. Nor is the dimension a stretch of space as ordinarily understood; for everything spatial, as something for which space is made, is already in need of the dimension, that is, that into which it is admitted.

The nature of the dimension is the meting out—which is cleared and so can be spanned—of the between: the upward to the sky as well as the downward to the earth.[10]

This passage can provide us with a transition to a consideration of the Fourfold.

The Fourfold   13

We stated that the late names for being are relational. They no longer designate a being in any possible sense of that word, but a relation that is prior to its relata. We have still not yet managed to elucidate that meaning of the term 'relation'. It is most clearly explicated in *Identity and Difference* as the belonging together of man and being. Perhaps the most potent sense of the finitude of being lies in the fact that being needs and uses (*braucht*) man.

The Fourfold, however, is an even richer name for being than is Appropriation, the belonging together of man and being. It introduces something sorely neglected by almost all philosophers, including the early Heidegger himself: *nature*. It also includes the elements of divinity: the godlike ones (*die Göttlichen*). Finally, with the Fourfold, Heidegger tries to work out belonging together, to delineate the kind of relatedness. His rather odd-sounding name for that relation is the "mirror-play" (*Spiegel – Spiel*)[1].

The main difficulty with the Fourfold is that in order to think it appropriately, one would have to start with the Fourfold as such and from there first consider its four constituents. After all, Heidegger tells us repeatedly that the relation first determines its constituents. We, however, are unable to proceed in this appropriate manner and are forced to consider the constituents first. Otherwise, we would start out with the traditional preconception of what a relation is, which, in turn, would probably leave us with the traditional concepts of man and God. 'Nature' would then probably be swept under the representational carpet altogether or else relegated to the condescendingly suspect realm of the 'poetic'.

Nature   14

The elements of the Fourfold are, of course, earth and heaven, the godlike ones and the mortals. 'Nature' is constituted by earth and heaven. Consideration of nature and the gods was surely encouraged by Heidegger's work on Hölderlin. As Gadamer remarked, "It was Hölderlin who first freed his tongue."[1] The other catalyst at work here is, again, Schelling, whose philosophy of nature was in turn influenced by Jakob Böhme.

As is well known, Böhme often speaks of the Wheel of Nature or of Birth. This is one of his most profound insights through which he expresses the dualism of forces in Nature laboring with itself, striving to bring itself to birth, but unable to do so. But it is just he himself who really is this Wheel, he himself desires to give birth to this science but is unable to do so. . . . This circular motion of his spirit shows itself outwardly in the fact that in each of his writings Böhme again starts from the outset, again sets forth the often and sufficiently explained beginnings without ever moving ahead or getting to a new ground. In these beginnings he is always admirable, a true spectacle of Nature laboring with itself and yearning for freedom and autonomy but always remaining at the same spot, rotating about itself, unable to transform its rotation into real motion.[2]

This could almost be a self-description on Schelling's part. As far as beginnings go, there are three versions of the beginning of *Die Weltalter* (*The Ages of the World*), which was never completed. In that work, Schelling speaks of a wheel rotating about itself, never able to mesh in gear and really move. Heidegger himself mentions this same phenomenon when relating Nietzsche's thought of the eternal recurrence of the same to the essence of technology.

What else is the essence of modern electrical machines than a form of the eternal recurrence of the same?[3]

We do not mention Schelling and Böhme because we are trying to document Heidegger's derivativeness from them, but because we are trying to show that there is *some* precedence for Heidegger's tenacity in consistently emphasizing the rather baffling element of concealment.

We return to nature, to earth and heaven. We select as our initial text "The Origin of the Work of Art," although the opposition there is between earth and world, whereas world later becomes the term for the whole of the Fourfold. We shall see what Heidegger has to say in this essay about earth and then see if what he says about world corresponds to what he will later say about the heaven. We shall find that the conception of earth also changes, according to whether it is related to world or to heaven.

The Greeks early called this emerging and rising in itself and in all things *phusis*. It clears and illuminates, also, that on which and in which man bases his dwelling. We call this ground the *earth*. What this word says is not to be associated with the idea of a mass of matter deposited somewhere, or with the merely astronomical idea of a planet. Earth is that whence the arising brings back and shelters everything that arises without violation. In the things that arise, earth is present as the sheltering agent.[4]

By earth, Heidegger means neither the soil that we can see and touch nor the planet bearing that name. Rather, earth is closer to being a principle than to being an element, if we are able to think 'principle' not as an abstract law but as a concrete movement. 'Abstract' and 'concrete' are terms thoroughly branded by metaphysics and are out of place here. The main thing to avoid is thinking something universal (*koinon*) which subsumes a variety of examples.

Earth is the principle of self-closing and self-seclusion. This self-seclusion is essential; it is not to be tampered with. Heidegger gives the example of a rock. The rock is through and through opaque, obdurately impenetrable to sight and knowledge. If I smash the rock in an attempt to see what is "inside," I am left with fragments of rock; nothing has been revealed. We now move on to world.

The world is not the mere collection of the countable or uncountable, familiar and unfamiliar things that are just there.

But neither is it a merely imagined framework added by our representation to the sum of such given things. The *world worlds,* and is more fully in being than the tangible and perceptible realm in which we believe ourselves to be at home.[5]

From the very beginning, Heidegger has always had a great deal to say about world. The concept of world has always been highly useful for him in getting away from the subject–object structure of experience, in dispensing with an 'over against'. World is closer to an 'around' or a context than it is to being any kind of thing.

The world grounds itself on the earth and earth juts through world. But the relation between world and earth does not wither away into the empty unity of opposites unconcerned with one another. The world, in resting upon the earth, strives to surmount it. As self-opening it cannot endure anything closed. The earth, however, as sheltering and concealing, tends always to draw the world into itself and keep it there. The opposition of world and earth is a striving.[6]

Here we clearly see the strife of concealment and unconcealment at work. We also see the same ambiguity in concealment that we have been discussing: concealment is at the same time refusal or dissembling and sheltering. But in the art work, earth cannot simply be equated with concealment and world with unconcealment.

But the world is not simply the Open that corresponds to clearing, and the earth is not simply the Closed that corresponds to concealment. Rather, the world is the clearing of the paths of essential guiding directions with which all decision complies. Every decision, however, bases itself on something not mastered, something concealed, confusing; else it would never be a decision. The earth is not simply the Closed, but rather that which rises up as self-closing.[7]

The earth *rises up* as self-closing. Concealment is revealed as such. Thus, it is not *total* concealment, but concealment revealed. And world is never total unconcealment. *In itself* it contains an element of concealment, not only in strife with earth or concealment. The best "example" of this would be the Chinese emblem of yin-yang, where a white and a black half are nestled against each other in a circle with the white half containing a small black circle and the black half containing a small white circle.

In the later essays "Building Dwelling Thinking" and "The Thing," world has disappeared as a separate element and become a name for the whole Fourfold. What takes its place is the heaven. Similarly, earth undergoes a fairly substantial shift of meaning.

Earth is the serving bearer, blossoming and fruiting, spreading out in rock and water, rising up into plant and animal.[8]

Earth is the building bearer, nourishing with its fruits, tending water and rock, plant and animal.[9]

Earth has relinquished the character of concealing. It is now closer to Heidegger's use of the word *ground* in *Beiträge:* that in and upon which something rests.

What has happened in the shift from world to the heaven?

The sky is the vaulting path of the sun, the course of the changing moon, the wandering glitter of the stars, the year's seasons and their changes, the light and dusk of day, the gloom and glow of night, the clemency and inclemency of the weather, the drifting clouds and blue depth of the ether.[10]

The "principle" of earth is broadly enough conceived to include water, rock, plant, and animal. It is Heidegger's reappropriation of the Greek *phusis,* nature, what arises and emerges of itself. Actually it goes back to the Presocratics: Thales' water, Anaximenes' air, Heraclitus's fire. The one element they left out, earth, Heidegger now introduces. As an example of a "speculative" treatment of an element, a passage from *"Aletheia"* might be adduced.

Therefore, the essence of the fire which Heraclitus *thinks* is not as transparently obvious as the image of a glowing flame might suggest. We need only heed ordinary, usage which speaks the word *pur* from diverse perspectives and thereby points toward the essential fullness of what is intimated in the thoughtful saying of the word.

Pur names the sacrificial fire, the oven's fire, the campfire, but also the glow of a torch, the scintillation of the stars. In 'fire,' lightning, glowing, blazing, soft shining hold sway and that which opens an expanse in brightness. In 'fire,' however, consuming, welding, cauterizing, extinguishing also reign.

When Heraclitus speaks of fire, he is primarily thinking of the lighting governance, the direction [*das Weisen*] which gives measure and takes it away.[11]

Yet earth is not the whole of nature. Its complement and counterpart is the heaven. The heaven is no longer primarily related to revealing and disclosing as was world. The heaven includes sun and moon with their concomitant changes of day and night and the seasons. The changes in the heaven bring about changes in the earth, which undergoes the shift of day and night and the seasons. Earth and heaven are inseparably interrelated, as are mortals and the godlike ones. After a brief look at these last two, mortals and the godlike ones, we shall try to consider the *relation* of the Fourfold itself.

In contrast to earth and the heaven, mortals and the godlike ones
are not confined to the context of the Fourfold. Beginning with the
Da-sein of *Being and Time,* human being has always been a prime
focus in Heidegger's thought. Predominantly in the writings on
Hölderlin and in *Beiträge,* the gods have always been a somewhat
cautious and reticent theme for Heidegger. Since these two extremely important factors in the Fourfold are so wide-ranging, and
since they are not the primary focus of our inquiry into finitude, we
shall just touch upon them here. We shall return to them in the context of a subsequent discussion of *Beiträge.*

> The divinities are the beckoning messengers of the godhead.
> Out of the holy sway of the godhead, the god appears in his
> presence or withdraws into his concealment.[1]

> The divinities are the beckoning messengers of the godhead.
> Out of the hidden sway of the divinities the god emerges as
> what he is, which removes him from any comparison with be-
> ings that are present.[2]

Heidegger makes no consistent distinction between the divinities (*die Göttlichen*), the godhead, the gods, the god, and the holy.
The term he uses as a name in the Fourfold, the 'divinities' or the
'godlike ones', is apparently of his own coinage. So is the term the
'godhead-like' (*das Gottheitliche*) in *Nietzsche II.* The 'godhead', a
term used by Eckhart to designate the transpersonal ultimacy of
the divine, Heidegger pretty much retains in that significance. The
holy is sometimes used as a harbinger of the god or the gods, sometimes as something beyond the gods. Since it is a term favored
by Hölderlin, it occupies a special place in Heidegger as well. There
is never a clear-cut distinction made between the god (monotheis-
tic) and the gods (polytheistic). However, we can safely say that

Heidegger does not have the god of Judeo-Christianity in mind, particularly not the philosophical conception of that god.

Finally, there are mortals who provide the access to the Fourfold while remaining one of its constituents.

> The mortals are the human beings. They are called mortals
> because they can die. To die means to be capable of death *as*
> death. Only man dies, and indeed continually, as long as he re-
> mains on earth, under the sky, before the divinities.[3]

The emphasis on death, already present in *Being and Time*,
is put in a less 'existential', more 'poetic' and enigmatic context.
Death is the shrine of nothingness, the shelter of being (*das Gebirg
des Seins*).

> Death is the shrine of Nothing, that is, of that which in every
> respect is never something that merely exists, but which nev-
> ertheless presences, even as the mystery of being itself. As
> the shrine of Nothing, death harbors within itself the presenc-
> ing of being. As the shrine of Nothing, death is the shelter
> of being. We now call mortals mortals—not because their
> earthly life comes to an end, but because they are capable of
> death as death. Mortals are who they are, as mortals, present
> in the shelter of being. They are the presencing relation to be-
> ing as being.[4]

Having barely sketched out the members of the Fourfold, we
now attempt to look at the Fourfold itself, the unity of the four.
To sum up, earth is not the earth of geology or geography, the
heaven is not the heaven of astronomy, the godlike ones do not coincide with the Judeo-Christian creator god, and the mortals are
not rational animals.

The manner of relatedness of the four members of the Fourfold
is named with three names: the pure draft (*Bezug*), the in-finite relation, and mirror-play. The first name is borrowed from Rilke, the
second, from Hölderlin, and the third is Heidegger's own.

The Pure Draft   **16**

We must bear in mind that Heidegger has reservations about Rilke since he remains within the realm of the completion of metaphysics taking place with Nietzsche. That means that being is conceived as will. To that extent, in this context, Heidegger is still diagnosing the current form of being as the will to will. Yet, within that context Heidegger is trying to get at the pristine meaning of relation (*Bezug*), which Hofstadter here aptly translates as draft or pull. The relation is one that draws, attracts, and pulls.

> We are not in a position—or if we are, then only rarely and just barely—to experience purely in its own terms a relation that obtains between two things, two beings. We immediately conceive the relation in terms of the things which in the given instance are related. We little understand how, in what way, by what means, and from where the relation comes about and what it properly is *qua* relation.[1]

One searches in vain for a concrete "example" of what Heidegger is thinking here: a relation which first determines the things or beings related. He is not thinking a general rule capable of subsuming specific examples, but something utterly unique. To begin with, the language in Rilke's poem describes a play of *forces:* the draft, the force of gravity. We are dealing not with things but with occurrences. Thus, the relation at stake here cannot be thought in the habitual way.

> Indeed, the expression "the whole *Bezug*," is completely unthinkable if *Bezug* is represented as mere relation.[2]

Another, indeed more central, term for *Bezug* (the draft) is the 'Open'. It is absolutely crucial to discern the difference between Rilke's Open and Heidegger's Open (*das Offene*) or clearing (*die*

Lichtung). Heidegger himself was very concerned about emphasizing the difference and was surprisingly acrid in his criticism of Rilke's poetic term.

> What Rilke designates by this term (the Open) is not in any way defined by openness in the sense of the unconcealedness of beings that lets beings as such be present. If we attempted to interpret what Rilke has in mind as the Open in the sense of unconcealedness and what is unconcealed, we would have to say: what Rilke experiences as the Open is precisely what is closed up, unlightened, which draws on in boundlessness, so that it is incapable of encountering anything unusual, or indeed anything at all.[3]

How can Heidegger assert that Rilke's Open is precisely what is closed up? His main criticism of Rilke's Open is clear: It has no limits or boundaries. Here Heidegger adheres to his roots in Greek thought: to be means to be something definite, defined, and limited. Infinity is equivalent with nonbeing. But how can what has no limits be *closed off*?

We get no answer from Heidegger himself. Having asserted that Rilke's Open is closed off, he goes into a detailed analysis of degrees of consciousness, of the specific difference between animal and human being. Pursuing that question would lead us away from our question about Rilke's poetic conception of the Open and Heidegger's adamant criticism of it.

Discussing Rilke's Open, Heidegger says:

> Beings advance and transit to beings. Only this advancing 'is,' but it 'is' only in forgetting the 'is' itself and its essence. This unlimited advancing of beings following and mingling with each other is supposed to be 'being.' This unlimited advance from beings to beings then points to 'the Open' in the sense in which we speak of the 'open sea' when the high seas have been reached in which all the boundaries of land have disappeared.[4]

The only possible meaning of being closed off would have to be that Rilke's Open is closed off *from being*. It remains trapped in the realm of beings, providing a kind of emptiness that permits beings to advance endlessly, transiting to and mingling with each other. This is a rather hopeless, if not demonic, situation.

Understandably, from his point of view, Heidegger objects vigorously to Rilke's eighth *Duino Elegy* which ascribes to the animal direct access to the Open. On the contrary, Heidegger asserts that only man has access to unconcealment as the Open, and this Open or unconcealment is separated from what Rilke means by the term by an 'abyss'. Heidegger calls Rilke's view "botched Christianity."

Whether or not Heidegger does justice to Rilke's poem cannot concern us here. However, the possibility remains that Rilke saw something here that Heidegger could not or would not.

Heidegger then analyzes Rilke's 'solution', within the limits of his metaphysics, to man's problem. Plant and animal are admitted into the Open; they remain in the drawing of the pure draft because they do not represent and objectify. Man, however, is excluded from the Open of the pure draft. Not only that, he makes things worse by reordering and reframing the world, forcing it under his domination. Man's self-assertion results in a parting, not *from,* but *against* the Open of the pure draft.

We shall assume some familiarity with Heidegger's writings on technology and conclude our discussion of the pure, whole draft with an indication of the solution, again within the restrictions of metaphysics, to man's predicament. How can man gain admittance to the pure draft?

Man is *unprotected;* but by a kind of conversion he can attain a *safety.*

> A safety exists only outside the objectifying turning away from the Open, 'outside all caring,' outside the parting against the pure draft. . . . To be secure is to repose safely within the drawing of the whole draft.[5]

> The daring that is more venturesome, willing more strongly than any self-assertion, because it is willing, 'creates' a secureness for us in the Open.[6]

In this context, the 'venture' is a metaphysical name for the being of beings. In contrast to plant and animal, man is more venturesome in that he goes *with* the venture. The quality of his consciousness, his self-consciousness, makes him more daring and venturesome. When his being more venturesome takes the form of self-assertion, he parts against the Open. If that self-assertion can be *converted,* turned around from self-assertion to being willing (*willig*), he can gain access to the Open of the pure draft. To be willing means to be compliant, to accede to turning toward the Open of the pure draft instead of against it. Instead of asserting himself, man can willingly let things be.

The distinctive feature of the conversion consists in our having seen unshieldedness as what is threatening us. Only such a having-seen sees the danger. It sees that unshieldedness as such threatens our nature with the loss of our belonging to the Open. The conversion must lie in this having-seen. It is then that unshieldedness is turned into the Open. By having seen the danger as the threat to our human being, we must have accomplished the inversion of the parting against the Open. This implies: the Open itself must have turned toward us in a way that allows us to turn our unshieldedness toward it.[7]

When we are able to see that the quality of our consciousness, our representing, objectifying, and calculating everything, threatens us with the loss of our belonging to the Open, we can put a stop to the self-assertion that has distorted our true nature and everything else along with it. The Open cannot turn toward us until we cease turning against it. We must simply stop interfering with everything and let things be what they are.

Represented in terms of Rilke's metaphysical orientation, turning unshieldedness into the Open of the pure draft is the task of the poet. It is the answer to the question experienced in the title of the essay "What Are Poets For?" But for Rilke himself, it will be the Angel.

How, specifically, does turning unshieldedness into the Open of the pure draft come about?

> But since the turning of unshieldedness into the Open concerns the nature of unshieldedness from the very start, this conversion of unshieldedness is a conversion of consciousness, and that *inside* the sphere of consciousness. The sphere of the invisible and interior determines the nature of unshieldedness, but also the manner in which it is turned into the widest orbit. Thus, that toward which the essentially inner and invisible must turn to find its own can itself only be the most invisible of the invisible and the innermost of the inner.[8]

From this passage we can see what for Heidegger is metaphysical about Rilke. First of all, he is speaking of 'consciousness', a term of modern metaphysics which Heidegger scrupulously avoided from the outset. Secondly, the separation of the visible from the invisible goes back to Plato's divided line in Book VI of *The Republic* and, beyond that, perhaps even to Heraclitus (hidden harmony is stronger than visible harmony) and Parmenides (truth and opinion).

For Rilke, we must turn and convert from the visible realm of willing and objectifying to the invisible realm of the innermost region of the Heart's space. Citing Pascal's distinction between the logic of reason (*l'esprit de la geometrie*) and the logic of the heart (*l'esprit du coeur*), Heidegger takes the heart to be close to the German *Gemüt,* an untranslatable word for the whole human being, not just for calculating reason. Heidegger deliberately mistranslates *l'esprit* as logic, instead of as spirit, to drive his point home more effectively. We must transmute what is visible in representation and calculation to what is invisible in the heart. Heidegger cites from Rilke's *Letters from Muzot:*

> The Angel of the *Elegies* is that creature in whom the transmutation of the visible into the invisible, which we achieve, seems already accomplished. The Angel of the *Elegies* is that being who assures the recognition of a higher order of reality in the invisible.[9]

The higher order of reality in the invisible is beyond the vicissitudes and confusion of the visible realm. Plant and animal are lulled into the Open by their drives. The Angel, whose nature it is to be bodiless, is no longer lured into the confusion incurred by what is sensibly visible. The realm of the visible is essentially the realm of the *unstilled.*

> The balance of danger then passes out of the realm of calculating will over to the Angel, . . .

> . . . When from the merchant's hand
> the balance passes over
> to that Angel who, in the heavens,
> stills it, appeases it by the equalizing of space.

> The equalizing space is the world's inner space, in that it gives space to the worldly whole of the Open. Thus the space grants to the one and to the other draft the appearance of their unifying oneness.[10]

The other draft is the other side of the whole draft of the Open, the aspect of life that is averted from us, similar to the side of the moon that we cannot see. The Angel is the being who is drawn by both sides of the whole draft and who has already accomplished the transmutation of what is visible in representation into that which is an invisible of the heart. When the balance of danger passes from the realm of calculating will over to the Angel, the parting against the Open and its unwholesomeness is converted into a sound whole. Spoken within the language of metaphysics, Rilke's answer to the often-quoted lines from Hölderlin; "But where there is danger, there grows also what saves," is that it is the Angel who can restore wholeness and the holy. He can heal the rift between the visible and the invisible, between the pure draft of the Open and its other side, by stilling the inconstancy brought about by the parting against the Open that objectifies and distorts everything. For Heidegger, who distances himself from what he considers to be Rilke's poetic metaphysics, the formulation of what saves translates into the poet's saying.

The In-finite Relation (*Verhältnis*)

Of the three terms for the relation of the four members of the Four-fold, the only one about which Heidegger has no reservations is his own term, the 'mirror-play' of the Fourfold. Whereas Rilke's conception of the pure draft is tainted by metaphysics, Hölderlin's in-finite relation is jeopardized by its proximity to the dialectic of German Idealism with which he grew up. His "roommates" in the seminary at Tübingen were, after all, Hegel and Schelling.

We have already stated that Heidegger has absolutely no use for the conception of infinity as the boundless and endless. He seems to consider that some kind of derivative perversion of Judeo-Christianity.

Thus, in-finite for Heidegger cannot mean the boundless and endless.

We pay heed not only to the words 'real/whole relation, including the middle' and *suspect* them to be the name for that totality of earth and heaven, god and man. Following Hölderlin's 'Philosophical Fragments' from his early years in Homburg, we may call this 'whole relation' to which earth and heaven and their relation belong the 'more delicate infinite relation.' The determination '*in-finite*' is to be thought in the sense of Fichte's, Hegel's and Schelling's speculative dialectic.

In-finite means that the ends and sides, the regions of the relation do not stand cut off onesidedly by themselves; rather freed of one-sidedness and finitude, they belong infinitely to each other in the relation that 'thoroughly' holds them together from out of its middle. The middle, which is so called because it mediates, is neither earth nor heaven, neither god nor man. The in-finite to be thought here differs abysmally from the mere endless that admits of no growth because of its uniformity. On the contrary, the 'more delicate relation' of earth and heaven, god and man can become more in-finite.

For what is not onesided can more purely appear out of the intimacy in which the four are held toward each other.[1]

Heidegger takes the fundamental term of German Idealism 'mediation', and reinterprets it in a nonmetaphysical way. For the German Idealists, mediation took place as the *movement* of the mediation of opposites: in the best known formulation of Hegel, from 'in itself' to 'for itself' to 'in and for itself'. In this process the opposites *pass over into* each other, losing their limited one-sidedness, preserving their essential being, and being elevated to a higher level of reality. This is the process of dialectic.

How does the mediation thought by Hölderlin, and with him Heidegger, differ from that dialectic? This nonmetaphysical, nondialectical (in the traditional sense) mediation is determined solely by the *middle*. The middle is not a point equidistant from two sides; rather, the middle releases the sides from itself and holds them apart and toward each other. The middle's releasing is its mediation as sending. The middle sends the heaven, earth, man, and the god to each other in keeping them gathered to itself.

'Four' does not name a calculated sum, but the form, unifying from out of itself, of the infinite relation of the voices of the sending. And the sending itself? What do the sending's voices tell us about it? It sends the four to each other by keeping them, the whole relation, gathered to itself. Then the sending would presumably be 'the middle' that mediates by first mediating and sending the four into their belonging together. The sending fetches the four to itself in its middle, incorporates them, initiates them into intimacy. . . . As the middle of the whole relation, the sending is the initiation (*An-fang*) that gathers everything. As the sonorous great sending, the middle is the great incipience (*Anfang*).[2]

With the word *Anfang*, Heidegger apparently wants to combine the meanings of beginning, incipience, or initiation with the literal meaning of catching or capturing. One could perhaps think of this as a bracing and gathering that releases a beginning, as when a sprinter gathers and collects himself before beginning his run. Contraction begets expansion.

But why is the sending of this incipience *sonorous?* Consistently avoiding any sort of visual representation, Heidegger keeps everything in the realm of sound here. We are not digressing with this discussion of sonorous. The sonorous is Heidegger's way of placing the problematic of mediation in the realm of sound, thus obviating anything representational and even dialectically oppositional.

The heaven sounds. It is one of the voices of the sending. Another voice is the earth, It, too, sounds.

The earth, sounding like on calf's skin. Just as the skin of the beaten drum echoes thunderingly the drumbeats in its way, the earth echoes in response to the strikes of the lightning and the 'arrow rain.' The earth's sounding is the heaven's echo. In the echo the earth answers to the heaven its own course.[3]

Not only heaven and earth are voices of the sending; the poet who gazes and calls out into immortality and the god, and the god himself, are also voices of the sending. Heaven, earth, man, and the god are all voices of the sending. But the earth has been taken over by industrial and technological organization, and even the heaven is being exploited by expeditions into cosmic space.

The earth and heaven of the poem have disappeared. Who would dare to say whereto? The in-finite relation of earth and heaven, man and god seems to have been destroyed. Or has it never yet appeared out of the gathering of the attuned sending *as* this in-finite relation purely joined in our history, never yet become present, never yet established as the whole in the highest of art? Then it could not be destroyed, but in the most extreme case only distorted and denied its appearance. Then it would be up to us to reflect upon this denial of the in-finite relation.[4]

Earth and heaven, the gods and mortals are destined to presence as the in-finite relation. But they have been denied their presencing through the technological transformation and exploitation of the earth and heaven. Yet they are only distorted, not destroyed. What is now lacking are their voices through which they call, reach, and attune us.

Manipulation has flattened down the structure of the infinite relation. Their interdependence (*Zueinander*) no longer sounds. The challenge of everything that is and can be into calculating ordering *distorts* the in-finite relation. Still more: the challenge reigning in the dominance of the essence of modern technology keeps That in the realm of the unexperienceable

whence the directing power of the challenge receives its destiny. What is that? It is the middle of the whole infinite relation. The middle is the pure sending itself. Something uncanny
is rotating around the globe: the fact that the sending now
reaches the men of this age *immediately,* not first through the
sounding of its voices. The sending reaches man soundlessly—
an enigmatic kind of stillness. Man will presumably fail to
hear that stillness for a long time. Thus he is unable to co-
respond to the destiny of denial. Rather, he evades it by his attempts, ever more hopeless, to master technology with his
mortal will.[5]

Instead of constituting a dialectical process, the mediation
thought by Heidegger tempers the relation of earth and heaven,
gods and man to each other, and thus mitigates and alleviates what
would be overpowering if experienced directly. The fact that the essence of technology has now silenced these voices constitutes the
danger of our present time.

   Just as Heidegger found the philosophical designations of
immanence and transcendence ultimately inadequate to characterize being, he now attempts to think an 'in-finite', which is neither
finite nor infinite in the traditional sense. The relation of earth
and heaven, gods and mortals is between four realms; thus, it is
not numberless. But these are *realms,* not things or beings; thus,
they are not limited in the way that objectively present things
are limited.

   In general, what Heidegger calls "the holy," and also "the
Open," is conceived as immediate and, as such, too excessive to be
immediately accessible.

The Open itself, however, which first gives to all toward-and-
together-with-each-other the realm in which they belong to
each other does not come from mediation. The Open itself is
the immediate. Thus nothing mediate, whether it be a god or
a man, is able to reach the immediate immediately.[6]

The Open or the holy is 'something' inviolate and inviolable
that will suffer no direct approach. Neither the gods nor man is able
to bring about an immediate relation to it. For this the poet, also
called the demigod, is necessary.

Now they (the poets) must stand where the holy itself, more
prepared and initially, opens itself. The poets must leave its

immediacy to the immediate and yet at the same time take over its mediation as the unique. Thus it is their dignity and duty to remain in relation to the higher mediators (the gods). Now that the dawn has come the 'burden of failure' is not lessened, but increased to the scarcely endurable. Although the immediate can never be immediately perceived, they yet must grasp the mediating stream 'with their own hands' and persevere even in the 'insurgence' (*Wettern*) of the rising incipience.[7]

Somehow, in some inexplicable way, the poet is able to grasp the stream of the immediate and congeal it, so to speak, into the word, the poem.

We turn now to the third characterization of the relation, the mirror-play of the Fourfold.

The "members" of the Fourfold are not four *things* standing in relation to each other. They are four possible presencings that 'are' only when they presence in the thing. The heaven is not 'up there' and the earth 'down here'. Heaven and earth presence in the thing; apart from that presencing we cannot say that they are. Presumably, Heidegger conceives the thing broadly enough to encompass, for example, a flower or a tree. He discusses a jug and a bridge as examples of a thing gathering the Fourfold. They are well suited to his purpose in that they emphasize the building and producing of mortals.

That the Fourfold may not be conceived as constituted by four things is perhaps best elucidated by thinking of world. The Fourfold names world. World is in no sense of the word a thing. World always names the whole, not abstractly, but concretely. This can be illustrated by the different magazines one sees on newspaper stands: *Computer World, The World of Sports, The World of Fashion,* etc. World and the Fourfold presence in the thing. They cannot be permanently located in, or identified with, the thing.

Thus, the Fourfold is the opposite of any kind of objective presence (*Vorhandenheit*). It is similar to the experience of totality or the whole. The whole is never objectively present and as such accessible to experience. I can never experience the whole "quantitatively" by traversing the entire earth. The very discursiveness of my traversing would dissipate the experience of totality. I must experience totality qualitatively, in some moment which embraces everything. This kind of experience is described by two of our poets, Tennyson and Blake. Tennyson spoke of the flower in the crannied wall which, if I could understand or experience it wholly, would enable me to understand everything. Blake actually had the experience of totality when he wrote of infinity in the palm of his hand and eternity in an hour.

How, then, does the Fourfold presence? As mirror-play. Still trying to think a relation instead of a substantial thing or being,

Heidegger introduces the context of world and thing. He wants to think relation as the nonmetaphysical difference between world and thing. What started out as the ontological difference between being and beings now becomes the difference between world and thing. We have already discussed this to some extent as *Austrag,* perdurance.

> It will not be possible to think Appropriation with the help of the concepts of being and the history of being; nor with the help of the Greek (one must rather 'go beyond' it). Along with the concept of being, the ontological difference disappears, too. In anticipation one would have to view the continuous reference to the ontological difference from 1927 to 1936 as a necessary blind alley (*Holzweg*).[1]

In the nonontological difference, world has taken the place of being and thing has taken the place of beings. World is the Fourfold which presences in the thing. World and thing span out and measure through a middle, a between that is the difference.

> The dif-ference is neither distinction nor relation. The difference is, at most, dimension for world and thing. But in this case 'dimension' also no longer means a precinct already present independently in which this or that comes to settle. The dif-ference is *the* dimension, insofar as it measures out, apportions, world and thing, each to its own. Its allotment of them first opens up the separateness and towardness of world and thing. Such an opening up is the way in which the difference here spans the two. The dif-ference, as the middle for world and things, metes out the measure of their presence. In the bidding that calls thing and world, what is really called is: the dif-ference.[2]

The Fourfold presences in the thing. World as the Fourfold has been "deconstructed" into four world-regions (*Weltgegenden*), and the thing has been deobjectified as the 'place' in which the world regions can presence. The Fourfold presences in the thing as the mirror-play.

Again, in the interest of intelligibility, we ask, Is there any sort of remote precedence for the components of this expression? Play, as the alternative possibility of describing the occurrence of world to mechanism and teleology, has at least two predecessors: Heraclitus and Nietzsche. Play is outside of all causality, be it mechanical, efficient causality or teleological, purpose-oriented causality. In much of German literature of the eighteenth and nineteenth century, play was considered the highest form of free activity.

The only predecessor who comes to mind for mirror is Leibniz.

Now this interconnection, relationship, or this adaptation of all things to each particular one, and of each one to all the rest, brings it about that every simple substance has relations which express all the others and that it is consequently a perpetual living mirror of the universe.[3]

Heidegger is trying to think a nonmetaphysical sense of reflection. Here reflection has little to do with thinking or pondering; it is not *"bent back"* in a relation to the thinking ego, but *throws* back an image in the way that a mirror throws my image back at me. The difference between this example and what Heidegger is trying to think is that it is not an image that is thrown back here.

Each of the four mirrors in its own way the presence of the others. Each therewith reflects itself into its own, with the simpleness of the four. This mirroring does not portray a likeness. The mirroring, lightening each of the four, appropriates their own presencing into simple belonging to one another. Mirroring in this appropriating-lightening way, each of the four plays to each of the others. The appropriative mirroring sets each of the four free into its own, but it binds these free ones into the simplicity of their essential being toward one another.[4]

Each of the four reflects, mirrors, itself to the others. This mirroring does not transmit a mere mirror image; it clears each of the four and appropriates them to each other. 'Clearing' in this context seems to mean something like set free, release. This setting free and releasing does not just cut each of the four loose, but releases them into their intimate belonging together.

None of the four insists on its own separate particularity. Rather, each is expropriated within their mutual appropriation into its own being. This expropriative appropriating is the mirror-play of the Fourfold.[5]

What does the phrase "expropriative appropriating" mean? Again, we have an adjective that appears to negate the noun it modifies. This should not leave us with nothing at all, but should modify the meaning of the noun. Thus, "expropriative appropriating" could mean an appropriating which is freed from the tendency to insist upon its own separate particularity or, for that matter, its own substantiality. This describes the activity of the Fourfold.

We must ask, What does a mirror do? A mirror by itself has no shape or image in it; it is empty. Because it is itself empty, it is able to reflect and give back the image of whatever comes before it.

However, the mirror of the mirror-play precisely does not mirror something standing before it; it mirrors itself. How is this possible and what does it mean?

Mirroring itself expropriates each realm into its own being. This expropriation has no image or likeness. It does not reflect the image of something in front of it, but bends and returns itself into its own being.

This is hardly the ordinary function of a mirror. It does not reflect an image. Nor does it *cause* anything; none of the four realms causes the others.

> The mirror-play of the worlding world, as the ringing of the ring, wrests free the united four into their own compliancy, the circling compliancy of their presence. Out of the ringing mirror-play the thinging of the thing takes place.[6]

The negating factor at work here begins to come more into focus. The German *ringen* means to ring, as in sound, and to wrestle. The meaning of sound takes it out of the domain of image and objectification. The negation of *ringen, entringen,* means to wrestle something *free.* The negating prefix *ent-* does not negate the meaning of ringing and wrestling, but indicates the *direction* in which the struggle moves. Similarly, *enteignen,* expropriating, does not negate appropriating but indicates a deeper level and dimension of appropriating: away from the stubborn insistence on the idiosyncratic in the direction of where the realm truly belongs and thus what it truly is.

> The thing stays—gathers and unites—the Fourfold. The thing—things world. Each thing stays the fourfold into a happening of the simple onehood of world.[7]

If we ask, Where is the Fourfold? the answer lies not in localizing these four realms in some area of world space. The answer is far simpler. The Fourfold presences in the thing and nowhere else. However, this 'simple' answer is extremely difficult to think and experience. Although Heidegger's examples of the thing in the essays "The Thing" and "Building Dwelling Thinking" were a jug and a bridge, his general intended meaning is by no means limited to things as products of man.

> Inconspicuously compliant is the thing: the jug and the bench, the footbridge and the plow. But tree and pond, too, brook and hill, are things, each in its own way. Things, each thinging from time to time in its own way, are heron and roe, deer, horse and bull. Things, each thinging and each staying in its own way, are mirror and clasp, book and picture, crown and cross.[8]

It is important to note the listing of what Heidegger did not develop elsewhere: animals and nature. In his eighth *Elegy*, Rilke saw an extraordinary presencing in the animal. Numberless poets, and most of us, can see presencing at work in a mountain, in trees and lakes. It is a bit harder to see it in an oil refinery.

Having ventured a short way into the Fourfold, we return to the consideration of being and Appropriation and their finitude. When Heidegger spells the German word for being, *das Sein,* in the older way as *das Seyn,* or when he crosses it out as ~~Sein~~, he means being now thought in a nonmetaphysical way. Here being is no longer thought as the ground of beings.

Eventually, we shall come back to our main question and conclude with whatever light we are able to throw on it: What does it mean that there is always concealment in the heart of being?

Years ago I myself wrote something to the effect that through concealment being saves itself from boundless unconcealment. No question as to what this actually means had arisen in my mind as yet. It made good logical sense. In the meantime, concealment has become more and more an enigma to me. I have already tried to consider some meanings of concealment in this study. Concealment can be preserving; it can be distorting. Yet this does not answer anything conclusively. I am not asking, Why is there concealment? for that would be asking for a rationalistic, ultimately metaphysical answer. But I am asking, What is the meaning of concealment? The background of that question is probably somewhat eschatological: Are we going to get stuck in the essence of technology, in Framing, or are we going to attain the Fourfold and Appropriation, the belonging together of man and being?

Our context now moves predominantly to *Beiträge,* a text unique in that it was not conceived as a lecture course or as a work in the traditional sense of that word.

> Future thinking is a *train of thought (Gedankengang)* through which the realm of the presencing of being concealed up to now is traversed and thus first cleared and attuned in the character of Appropriation most its own.[2]

The text brings ideas and formulations not found elsewhere. At times it is more hermetic than hermeneutic. In a way, it is less a *train* of thought than a *circling* around what he is trying to say. The subtitle to *Beiträge* is "On the Appropriation" (*Vom Ereignis*), indicating that, beginning in 1936 (the incipient year of writing the *Beiträge*), 'Appropriation' became the decisive word for being. Given the time in which *Beiträge* was written, 1936–38, it is inevitable that some of the later ideas and formulations—for example, the Fourfold inclusive of the heaven, not the world—had not yet been arrived at or worked out. With this one restriction, *Beiträge* contains a wealth of fascinating material to be studied.

We shall try to glean some insights from *Beiträge* that have not been exhaustively treated elsewhere, beginning with the question of the other beginning,[3] which is, to some extent, documented elsewhere. From there, we shall investigate what effect this other beginning might have on *Da-sein* and the gods. *Beiträge* contains some particularly enigmatic statements on the gods, most notably "the passing by of the last god."

The Other Beginning

Beiträge is divided into eight main sections: preview, assonance (*Anklang*), play (*Zuspiel*), leap, grounding, the future ones, the last god, and being. Most of this sounds a bit strange, to say the least. Preview speaks for itself; the last god and being will be discussed to some extent later. A brief, somewhat hesitant characterization of the other five terms with provisional translations might run as follows: assonance deals primarily with the first beginning as metaphysics. It is our legacy, the place from which we start. The play, as in the first *move* of a game (i.e., it is your play, move), is the other beginning, the new experience of being thrown and played to us by being (*das Zuspiel*). The remaining sections point forward to what follows from this play, the leap (elsewhere called "the step back") out of metaphysics into being as Appropriation. When the leap lands, first bringing about and constituting that land through its leaping, the task then becomes a grounding of the place of the moment (*Augenblicksstätte*) of being. That is to be accomplished and enacted by the future ones.

The title of the section where the two beginnings are predominantly discussed is the play (*das Zuspiel*). It is preceded by the section called assonance, sounding (*Anklang*). In general, Heidegger's preference for terms taken from the realm of sound is much in evidence in *Beiträge*. Not only are such terms not metaphysical, but they are completely removed from the realm of sight, possible objectification, and the target of much of Heidegger's polemic, Plato's *koinon* and *idea,* the universal Form or Idea.

What does Heidegger mean by assonance? What is assonance and what does it echo? Assonance is the resounding and resonance of an original sound. This resounding is the faint, distant remnant of the presencing of being in the abandonment of being. It must link up with the play in order to retrieve or recapitulate its own primordiality. The transition from the first beginning to the other beginning is constituted by the shift from the guiding question (*Leitfrage*) to the fundamental question (*Grundfrage*). The toss or play arches a bridge to another shore that is not yet determined and that is first decided and brought into being by the arching of the bridge.

The guiding question of the first beginning is, What are beings (*das Seiende,* to on)? The fundamental question is, What is the truth of being (*das Seyn*)?

The beginning of the transition from the first beginning to the other beginning is constituted by recognizing the fact that being has completely withdrawn itself and abandoned beings to manipulation (*Machenschaft*), manipulation being the forerunner of the later concept of framing. The danger lies not only in the fact that beings have been abandoned, but also in the fact that this very abandonment has been *forgotten*. This forgottenness not only constitutes the danger for being; above all, it creates a need in being itself which escalates into the need of needlessness, of a lack of need. Only when the need of needlessness is experienced and the abandonment of being is acknowledged and recognized is there any hope of a transition to the other beginning. This transition is not a continuous one but requires a leap.

Wherein does the difference between the leading question and the fundamental question consist?

> But the fundamental question as a formulated question (*gefasst*) also has a totally different character. It is not the continuation of the formulation of the guiding question in Aristotle. For it originates directly from a necessity of the need of the *abandonment of being,* that occurrence which is essentially co-conditioned by the history of the leading question and its failure to be recognized.[4]

When man can move from the tranquilized complacency of needlessness to an experience of the need submerged in this needlessness, he can move from the realm of the guiding question, dominant since Plato and Aristotle, to the realm of the fundamental question of the truth of being. He can experience the need of needlessness that is the abandonment of being. Until that happens, he will remain in thrall to manipulation and its corresponding attitude of 'thrill-seeking' (*Erlebnis*). Heidegger calls the either-or of this situation "the decision."

> All of these decisions that appear to be many and various can be reduced to a sole unique decision: whether being withdraws itself once and for all *or* whether this withdrawal as refusal becomes the first truth and the other beginning of history.[5]

In the later formulation: Do we get stuck in the essence of technology and Framing or does the Appropriation of man and being finally come about?

The first beginning is the entire history of being as metaphysics which did not and could not ask the question of the truth of being. Heidegger's formulations of the relation of the first beginning to the other beginning are complex and partly equivocal. What is clear beyond doubt is the fact that the first beginning's neglect of the question of the truth of being has resulted in the abandonment of being. Since we are not even aware of this abandonment, the abandonment has escalated to the forgottenness of being. As long as the abandonment of being remains forgotten, there is not only nothing that we can do, but we do not even realize that there is something to 'do'. The abandonment of being constitutes the need of being. The need of being escalates to the need of the needlessness of being through the forgottenness of the abandonment of being. The other beginning takes its origin in the realization of the forgottenness and the need of needlessness.

> The other beginning is not the opposite direction to the first, but *as an other* stands outside of opposition and immediate comparability. For this reason the dispute (*Auseinandersetzung*) is not a matter to be settled between opponents, neither in the sense of a rough dismissal nor in the manner of a supersession of the first beginning by the other one. With its new primordiality the other beginning helps the first beginning to the truth of its history and thus to the inalienable otherness most its own that only becomes fruitful in the historical dialogue of the thinkers.[6]

Da-sein

When the first beginning and its completion have been understood, and therewith the necessity of the other beginning, the guiding question of beings becomes the fundamental question of the truth of being. This brings about a profound transformation in human being.

From the very beginning, Heidegger has always polemicized vigorously against the concept of man, dominant ever since Aristotle, as the rational animal. Heidegger has always insisted that we do not know who or what man is. The reign of psychology and anthropology that metaphysically determines what became of Aristotle's concept of *zoon logon echon,* the animal or living being (physical) that has *logos* or reason (metaphysical) comes to an end with the completion of the first beginning.

Whereas the term *Dasein* in the first beginning meant existence in general, whether human or animal or whatever, *Da-sein* in the other beginning takes on a totally new cast.

The significance and matter of the word *Da-sein* is completely different in the thinking of the other beginning, so different that there is no mediating transition from that first usage to this other. *Da-sein* is not the kind of reality of any and every being, but is itself the being of the there. But the there is the openness of beings as such in the whole, the ground of the more primordially thought *aletheia. Da-sein* is a way to be which, in that it 'is' (actively and transitively, so to speak), the there, is a unique being (what presences in the presencing of being) in accordance with *this* distinctive being and as this being itself.

Da-sein is the ground, grounding itself, of the *aletheia* of *phusis,* the presencing of that openness which first opens self-concealing (the presencing of being) and is thus the truth of being itself.[7]

In the other beginning, *Da-sein* absolutely ceases to be the name for the existence and continuous presence and duration of anything, not even exclusively of human beings in the sense that Kierkegaard restricted existence to human existence, thus unwittingly becoming the founder of "existentialism." Kierkegaard himself would have objected strenuously to the coupling of existence with any "ism" since an "ism" implies a finished and closed system, whereas human existence is ever unfinished and fragmentary as long as it 'is'. Of the three most major thinkers lumped together under the label of existentialism—Kierkegaard, Heidegger, and Sartre—only Sartre espoused the term existential*ism*.

> In the sense of the other beginning *Da-sein* is what is still completely strange to us, something that we never come across, that we only bespring in the leap into the grounding of the openness of what conceals itself, that clearing of being into which future man must place himself in order to hold it open.[8]

The fact that *Da-sein* in the other beginning is never something that we come across means that it is never objectively present, never *there* as something enduring, persisting, and extended. This is an absolutely fundamental point that one wishes Heidegger had elaborated upon and developed more than he did. Perhaps he could not. Perhaps it cannot be done. He was, perhaps of necessity, more concerned with the *via negativa*, with distancing the overwhelmingly dominant idea, engendered and perpetuated by metaphysics, of static, enduring objects. Neither being nor *Da-sein* are objectively present, *always there*. They 'are' not; they presence. The presencing of the clearing for self-concealing, the phrase dominating *Beiträge* as its leitmotif, takes place in the place of the moment. All we can say, or all Heidegger was able to say, is that the clearing of self-concealing occurs suddenly and abruptly as the place of the moment, a phrase embodying Heidegger's new understanding of time and space as time-space. To ask where it was before the place of the moment occurs or what happens afterwards, the most natural questions in the world, is still inappropriate, based on the conception of enduring objective presence.

> In its turning the most intimate relation of being and *Da-sein* becomes visible as that which necessitates the fundamental question and forces us to actually go *beyond* the guiding question and thus beyond all metaphysics into the time-spatiality of the there.[9]

The fundamental question involves the time-spatiality of the there, time-space. A discussion of time-space leads us to the question of the a-byss and emptiness which we touched upon earlier. Taking that question up again, we can say that it is indeed a very complex one.

What is the a-byss? What is *its* manner of grounding? The a-byss is the staying-away of the ground. . . .
A-byss is staying-away; as ground in self-concealing, a self-concealing in the manner of the denial of the ground. However, denial is not nothing, but a distinctive primordial kind of leaving unfilled, empty; thus a distinctive kind of opening.[10]

Time-space grounds as the a-byss, as the staying away of the ground. The staying away of the ground allows an opening to originate.

A-byss is the hesitating denial of the ground. In the denial the primordial emptiness opens itself, the primordial *clearing* occurs, but at the same time the clearing in which hesitation shows itself.[11]

This emptiness or clearing is not to be thought in the traditional sense of pure space and time as empty containers with no content, or the Kantian forms of sensibility that remain when all else has been 'thought away'. Rather, self-concealing, hesitating denial, *shows* itself in the clearing. This is another formulation of the phrase running through *Beiträge* as a leitmotif: clearing for self-concealing. What shows itself in the clearing is self-concealing. This is the mystery, unveiled as mystery and no longer submerged in forgottenness. Hesitating denial is not a bald refusal; on the contrary, it is a beckoning (*Wink*).

The openness of the clearing of concealing is thus primordially not the mere emptiness of not being occupied, but the attuned and attuning emptiness of the a-byss which is attuned and that means here structured in accordance with the attuning beckoning of the Appropriation.[12]

The emptiness of the abyss is attuned and structured by the beckoning of the Appropriation. The thought expressed here is basically the same as that expressed by the term, the Open. Just as Heidegger decisively rejected Rilke's poetic conception of the Open because he felt it was without any bounds or limits, he here emphasizes that the emptiness of the a-byss is attuned and structured, that is, defined and definite.
To conclude this discussion of time-space (*Da-sein*), we need to take a look at the temporality and spatiality of hesitating self-withholding. We already know that temporality and spatiality by no

means coincide with the traditional concepts of time and space. That was already clear even in *Being and Time*.

Heidegger introduces the terms 'enrapturing', 'carrying off or away' (*Entrückung*) and 'taking in' (*Berückung*). The first term expresses movement and corresponds to time; the second involves a kind of stasis and corresponds to space.

> But self-denial denies itself hesitatingly; thus it gives the possibility of giving and appropriating. Self-denial structures the carrying off (rapture) of temporalizing; as *hesitating* it is at the same time the most primordial *taking in*. This taking in is the *encompassing* (*Umhalt*) in which the moment and thus temporality is held (like the *primordial* a-byss? Emptiness? Neither it nor fullness). This taking in allows the possibility of giving as presencing possibility, makes way for it. Taking in is the making way for Appropriation. Through taking in, abandonment stands fast and is to be *perdured.*[13]

Heidegger is attempting to express an extremely intricate and highly complex structural movement here. We cannot simply repeat his barely intelligible statements, but must try to clarify them without sacrificing any of the *essential* complexity. Whatever expressions we use in this process must of necessity remain inadequate and open to the misunderstandings that our metaphysically ingrained thinking perpetually falls into.

In our discussion of enrapturing (time) and taking in (space), we must keep in mind the basic framework of ground and abyss. Leaving the un-ground aside for the moment, we can put primal ground and ground together for the sake of simplicity and concentrate on the relation of ground and abyss (time-space). This relation is so dialectical (in the Heraclitean sense of oppositional) that it is nearly impossible to sort out a structure intelligible to our metaphysically conditioned way of thinking. But to some extent we need to retain that way of thinking as a kind of makeshift bridge or raft to where Heidegger stands. We would then no longer need the bridge or raft. A Kierkegaardian leap here would simply land us in sheer incomprehensibility. After all, Heidegger spoke of a *step* back (out of metaphysics).

If we can succeed in clarifying the relation of ground and abyss, we shall at least have succeeded in understanding something of Heidegger's insight. We must, of course, always bear in mind that the relation is what is primordial. The relata are always engendered and derivative. And nothing, absolutely nothing, is objectively present, statically enduring and persisting.

The ground presences as abyss. In order for presencing to be possible, there must be some sort of clearing or emptiness. If anything were already there, nothing (else) could presence. The ground must withhold its presencing, must refuse itself in hesitation, thus letting a clearing originate. This clearing is 'empty', but not empty in the sense of unoccupied space and time coordinates. The abyss arising from the ground's self-withholding is not mere emptiness or even chaos, but is 'constituted' as time-space. Self-withholding structures and makes possible the carrying off of temporalizing; it makes room for the activity and directionality of temporalizing by itself remaining absent, by refusing to presence. Since it is *hesitating* self-withholding, it provides a kind of *hold* instead of simply allowing a temporalizing that disperses itself into infinity. Whatever else it may be, Heidegger's ultimate insight is Greek, the affirmation of limit, definiteness and finitude is contradistinction to the Judeo-Christian affirmation of infinity and the infinite. To use more familiar language, one might say that temporalizing is centrifugal, whereas making room, encompassing (space), is centripetal. The 'center' is the beckoning of Appropriation in the other beginning.

This is Heidegger's "poetic" attempt to describe the activity of time as well as space, as opposed to representing them as static containers "in which" something, inexplicably, happens, takes place. With the expression "taking place" we have the unity of time and space understood as activities. Something *takes* (time) *place* (space). We have grown accustomed, since the latter part of the nineteenth century, to hearing about time as dynamic, as activity. Correcting his initial conception, in *Being and Time,* of space as derivative from time and as something basically inert, Heidegger is probably a true pioneer in trying to think the activity of space. It is not even enough to talk about dynamism and activity in general. Not content with general assertions, Heidegger is attempting to describe *how* time and space bring about presencing.

In a sense, Heidegger in his own way is dealing with the problem of avoiding extremes, the extremes known to Buddhism as permanence (*sasvata*) and nihilism (*uccheda*).

The avoidance of these two extremes is central to *all* forms of Buddhism and is one of the very few tenets, traceable to the Buddha himself, to be upheld despite many doctrinal disputes. The well-known characterization of Buddhism as the "Middle Way" is another expression of this tenet. It has both an ethical and an ontological level. The ethical level was experienced by the Buddha himself when he went from the one extreme in the luxury of his father's palace (eternalism, being) to the other extreme of asceticism where he nearly died of starvation (nihilism). He concluded that the best way to live was the middle way, avoiding the two extremes of luxury or eternalism and asceticism or nihilism.

On an ontological level, the Buddha refused to answer metaphysical questions such as whether the soul exists after death or not. To assert that the soul exists after death is to go against the Buddhist denial of a substantial soul or self (*atman*), and to encourage clinging to the belief in the immortality of the ego-self. To assert that the soul does not exist after death is to strike terror into the hearts of most people, land them in total despair, and foster nihilistic paralysis. Belief in either extreme, eternalism or nihilism, is a fatal hindrance.

Heidegger's formulation of these extremes takes on the form of objective presence (*Vorhandenheit*), or any kind of specific being whatsoever (*ein Seiendes*), versus nugatory nothingness (*das nichtige Nichts*). Being, what has not been thought in the history of metaphysics, is fundamentally what conceals itself (*das Sichverbergende*). If being did not conceal itself, it would presumably have to be thought and experienced as a being that is objectively present. Then we fall back into the trap of ontotheology and end up with being as the cause of the world and of itself and as the highest being. But Heidegger's being moves farther and farther away from anything like a cause and into the dimension of letting and sending. Whereas the Heidegger of *Being and Time* attempted to get away from substantivized beings or things by concentrating on the *relations between* (prepositions) those beings, the later Heidegger repeatedly tries to show how such a between or relation constitutes itself even before the things which it is between.

On the other hand, Heidegger is no nihilist. He *needs* nihilation and the nothing (the no-thing) in order to get away from substantializing and objectifying beings, and thus consistently states that the nothing belongs to the presencing of being. Given the choice, being is closer to nothing than to a being.

The same problem of avoiding extremes emerges in discussion of the ground. The section of *Beiträge* entitled "*Gründung*," "grounding," bears witness to Heidegger's struggle somehow to maintain the priority of the *relation* between man and being, here expressed as that between abyss and ground, without slipping back into the old metaphysics of saying that one thing causes or grounds another. The formulations here get so entangled, not to say contradictory, that the hermeneutical circle threatens to turn into a merry-go-round.

A previously quoted passage states that the a-byss is the remaining absent of the ground in self-concealing that occurs as the denial of the ground. But, we are told, denial is not nothing, but leaves unfilled and empty, thus permitting an opening to originate. Again, the thought expressed here is that the ground must stay away in order to permit an opening, a free space that, as Heidegger repeatedly emphasizes, is not simply general emptiness as a kind of indefinite absence, but a definite, specific emptiness. How can emptiness be definite and specific?

Emptiness can be defined by its surrounding boundaries if it has any; these boundaries then define it as *this* particular emptiness rather than something vague and indefinite. But this conception is dangerously close to the traditional idea of time and space as empty containers *in which* something can be or can occur to fill them. We would have to think the boundaries as inherently *belonging* to emptiness in order for it to be truly definite.

The *a*-byss is a-*byss*.[14] The a-byss remains inherently related to the ground. It is thus something specific, not general absence.

We pursue this thought a little further. If we persist, in spite of the barely intelligible intricacies of Heidegger's ponderings, the fundamental thought begins to be clear.

In that the ground still grounds precisely in the abyss, yet does not truly ground, it hesitates.

A-byss is the hesitating denial of the ground. In denial primordial emptiness opens itself, the primordial *clearing* occurs, but at the same time the clearing in which hesitation shows itself.

The a-byss is the first essential *clearing concealing*, the presencing of truth.[15]

The ground is not totally absent in the abyss, it is present in a hesitating manner. Ground and abyss are not all that far apart; they are not opposites. Ground cannot be equated with presence; abyss is not the same as absence. Heidegger has to think a presencing other than objective presence (*Vorhandenheit*) and an absence other than nugatory nothingness (*das nichtige Nichts, ouk on*). This is not an easy task.

Perhaps another way to approach the question of a definite emptiness is to think of the absence of a person close to us. This is hardly a general emptiness; rather, it is the most specific absence conceivable. This kind of absence can be overwhelming.

But since truth is the clearing concealing of being, as a-byss it is ground that grounds only as the Appropriation that bears and lets tower through (*als das tragende Durchragenlassen*). For hesitating denial is the beckoning in which *Da-sein*, the perdurance (*Beständnis*) of clearing concealing is beckoned, and that is the vibration of the turning between calling and belonging, the Appropriation, being itself.[16]

Grounding, a conception running throughout Heidegger's thought from "On the Essence of Ground" through *The Principle of Ground,* is to be thought, not as some kind of efficient cause, but as a letting tower through that bears and supports. The unusual expression "towering through" calls to mind Heidegger's use of the word *dimension,* not as a framework of coordinates, but literally as a kind of measuring through that does not measure something already there but first constitutes in its measuring through what it measures through.

Either-Or

It was, of course, Kierkegaard who put the phrase "either-or" on the philosophical map. His use of it was 'existential' in the genuine, poignant sense of the word before it was appropriated by Sartre. Heidegger's either-or goes beyond even the genuine sense of existential and might best be called "eschatological," if we can keep that term free of its traditional theological overtones. The "decision" at stake here is not primarily existential; it has to do with the destiny of being itself. We want to inquire into what it is about being that can involve it in an eschatological either-or, in a decision. This decision, of course, is not a matter of human deliberation and choice but is to be understood in a quasi-presocratic sense, like much of the later Heidegger, as a *separation* taking place in the path and destiny of being.

In *Beiträge,* Heidegger gives a whole list of either-ors which boil down to one fundamental one.

All these decisions that appear to be many and various contract into a single and unique one: whether being withdraws itself once and for all *or* whether this withdrawal as refusal becomes the first truth and the other beginning of history.[17]

This either-or will later get very clearly polarized, in *Identity and Difference,* into the alternatives: *Ereignis* (Appropriation) or *Gestell* (Framing). We shall return to this later position. For now, we shall explore what *Beiträge,* whose real title was to have been *Vom Ereignis (On the Appropriation),* has to say about either-or.

The truth of being is the being of truth—This expression sounds like an artificial and forced reversal, at best like an inducement to a dialectical game. But this reversal is only a fleeting and external sign of the turning *(Kehre)* presencing in being itself; it throws a light on what would here like to be called decision.[18]

The 'turn' *(Kehre)* is a much disputed term in the later Heidegger. Most often it is taken as a supposed turn in the direction of Heidegger's own thought, with varying speculations as to what precise date or just between which works this turn is to be located. Gadamer pluralizes the turn into turnings and compares them to the best way to get up a steep hill or mountain, that is, zig-zagging. We cannot and need not go into all that here. In our passage, Heidegger speaks of a "turning *presencing in being itself.*" In this use of the term 'turning' (and it is not the only one), the turning lies very close to strife, strife predominantly conceived in *Beiträge* as the strife between earth and world, occasionally between the gods and man. Written about the same time as "The Origin of the Work of Art," *Beiträge* still conceives strife as between earth and world. Later, the heaven will replace world in strife, rethought as play, with earth: these two are coordinated with man and the godlike ones, thus yielding the Fourfold. The Fourfold—earth, world, the godlike ones, and man—constitutes the *world.*

For 'being' does not mean here objective presence in itself, and nonbeing does not mean: complete disappearance, but nonbeing as a kind of being: in being and yet not; being, too: notlike and yet in being. Taking this back into the presencing of being requires the insight into the belonging of nothing to *being.* Thus the either-or receives its pointedness and its origin. Because being is notlike *(nichthaft),* it needs the perduring of the *nothing* for the perdurance of its truth and thus at the same time what is *against* everything notlike, unbeings *(das Unseiende).*

It follows from the essential notness of being (turning) that being requires and needs what from *Da-sein's* perspective shows itself as either-or.[19]

It appears to be the nothing that constitutes a certain oppositionality (strife) and turning in being itself and this oppositionality can, or perhaps must, potentiate itself into a decision.

This necessity enacts itself in the constant decision ruling all historical human being: whether man in the future will belong to the truth of being and thus shelter truth in beings out of this belonging and for its sake, or whether the incipience of the last man will drive him into displaced animality and deny the last god to historical man.[20]

The "last man" is drawn from Nietzsche's masterful description in *Thus Spoke Zarathustra* of the ineradicable ground-flea who hops around, blinks, and states, "We have found happiness."

In order to better understand the *relation* between the alternatives of this either-or—and the alternatives are by no means unrelated—we need to see what Heidegger says would have to happen if we are indeed to experience a more appropriate relation to being (i.e., to attain the other beginning). Only when the first beginning has reached its most extreme end does the other beginning come within the range of possibility. The often-quoted verse from Hölderlin expresses this most succinctly: "But where there is danger, there grows/also what saves."

This kind of turning or shift, the other beginning, represents a totally different processual direction which, nevertheless, can result only from the completed end of the first beginning. This is fairly clear and comprehensive. What is less clear is the turning within being itself, to which we shall return later.

Heidegger is most likely picking up on Nietzsche's play with the word *Notwendigkeit* here. *Notwendigkeit* is the customary word for necessity, which Nietzsche takes in its literal sense of "turning the need." Only from a profound and extreme need can the other beginning emerge. The most extreme need of all is the need of needlessness.

Expressed in terms of the headings of the sections in *Beiträge,* the transition from the first to the other beginning would go as follows:

The *assonance* of being as refusal.

The *play* of the questioning of being. The play is first of all the move, the play of the first beginning so that this beginning might bring the other beginning into play and from this reciprocal play the preparation of the leap might grow.

The *leap* into being. The leap besprings the abyss of the chasm and thus the necessity of the grounding of the *Da-sein* directed by being.

The *grounding* of truth as the truth of being (*Da-sein*).[21]

The first beginning must *resonate* into the next three 'stages' outlined by Heidegger. These stages are taken from "the as yet unassimilated fundamental outline of the historicity of the transition."[22] The assonance of being as refusal in the first beginning must resonate into the stages of the play, the leap, and the grounding. The play (*Zuspiel*) evokes the image of a move in a game that gives opportunity for and invites a response, an answering move. For example, in a chess game, the move of a pawn on the part of one player prompts the next move on the part of the other. Or in baseball, when the pitcher throws the ball, this is the opportunity for the batter to either hit it or miss it. The next stage is the leap, a leap which in the process of leaping first constitutes where it will land. There is no 'place' beforehand to which one could leap. Thus, it is not possible to anticipate or calculate where one will land. Strictly speaking, one cannot even say anything about the leap until one has taken it. Finally, the grounding stabilizes all this activity, brings it not to a halt but to its ground.

To return to the simpler, more readily comprehensible formulation of the transition from the first to the other beginning:

Assonance
of the presencing of being
from the abandonment of being
through the necessitating need
of the forgottenness of being.
By recollecting it *as* forgottenness to let this forgottenness appear in its concealed power and therein the assonance of being. *Recognizing* the need. . . .
The highest need: *the need of the lack of need.* . . . The assonance must encompass the totality of the rift and above all be fitted to the play as counterplay.

Assonance for whom? whereto? The assonance of the presencing of being in the abandonment of being. . . .
The final fixation of the abandonment of being in the forgottenness of being.[23]

Being has withdrawn itself; it remains absent. This constitutes the abandonment of being. Being has abandoned us. But we do not even realize this, and that constitutes the most extreme need. Were we but aware of the fact that there is a need, there would be some hope for a change. But all we are aware of is the lack of any need: needlessness.

Lack of need consists in believing that one has reality and what is real in one's grip and knows what truth is, without needing to know in what truth *presences*.[24]

We neglect and leave out being's abandonment and its remaining absent. This is the essence of nihilism.

This is all reasonably clear. As long as we are unable to see even that there is a need, nothing can happen. Even if something should happen, we wouldn't know it.

We need not go into the abandonment and forgottenness of being here to any great extent. It is described most incisively in *The End of Philosophy* and in the essays on technology. In *Beiträge*, Heidegger has not yet hit upon the term 'Gestell' (Framing) for the essence of technology and thus uses its preliminary formulation, 'machination' (*Machenschaft*), a term he later retained along with *Gestell*. Together with the description of machination, there is a lot of rather heated polemic against *Erlebnis* (thrill-seeking, experience). Machination and thrill-seeking belong together in the epoch of the completion of metaphysics and nihilism.

The assonance resonating from the first beginning that was concerned with the guiding question of beings continues on into the play that invites the possibility of the leap into being. With this leap the guiding question of beings is then transformed into the fundamental question of the truth of being.

Here, as well as elsewhere, there is a certain ambiguity in Heidegger's tone. On the one hand, he speaks of the other beginning and its development of the fundamental question as if this were already a reality, not just a possibility. His very speaking about it implies that he himself is, in some sense, already there in this other beginning. On the other hand, the either-or by no means disappears but remains as a genuinely undecided question.

Either get stuck in the end and its course and that means the renewed variations of 'metaphysics' that become more and more coarse, groundless and aimless (the new 'biologism' etc.), *or* begin the other beginning, i.e., be resolved for its long preparation.[25]

The first step toward the other beginning, if it is to occur at all, must be a transition from the lack of need to the immense need created by this lack of need. If we take a look at our own present-day society, we can observe all sorts of 'needs' being created by "business." Families have two or more cars, washing machines, dishwashers, microwave ovens, air conditioners, television sets, etc. If one goes to the supermarket, one is assaulted and overwhelmed by the inexhaustible variety of detergents, floor waxes, cereals, and every imaginable sort of food. These are hardly the sort of "needs" Heidegger is talking about. Even the poor people in this country, and especially in other parts of the world, who cannot afford these 'needs' and are therefore truly 'needy' do not have the kind of need at stake here. Heidegger is talking about something like (for lack of a better word) a "spiritual" need—a phrase he never uses. The answer to Nietzsche's diagnosis of the plight of the death of God does not appear to lie in an overman or in any other escalation of what we already have. The other beginning has to be truly *other,* even if it must preserve some continuity with the first.

The most extreme need is precisely the lack of need. Socrates' statement that he knew that he knew nothing can throw some light on this situation. In a certain sense, Socrates' statement is ironic in that he certainly doesn't believe that anyone else knows anything either, certainly not more than he. But in another, more essential sense, the statement is serious and straightforward. The kinds of things that Socrates wants to inquire into—knowledge, justice, beauty, immortality—neither he nor any other mortal really knows or can know exhaustively. Because Socrates *knows* that he does not know, he can *learn.* Anyone who thinks that he already knows will never learn anything; he is ineducable.

And so it is with the lack of need. If we are unable to experience a need, to see that there *is* a need, we shall continue on in the mindlessness of endless creature comforts which are, however, less innocuous than this term would imply.

The leap, as the question of the presencing of truth itself, first brings man into the play space of the onfall (*Anfall*) and the remaining absent of the arrival and flight of the gods. The other beginning wants only this. . . .

Not *proclamation* of new doctrines to a rigidified organization (*Betrieb*) of men, but *transposing* man out of the lack of need into the need of the lack of need as what is the most extreme need.[26]

The remaining topics of *Beiträge* that we wish to consider will be the turning in being itself, the question of instantaneity and the place of the moment, and, finally, again, self-concealment and finitude.

The Turning in Being Itself

The initial meaning of the term 'the turning', in the conception of *Being and Time,* was to start with human being, arrive at the meaning of being, and then turn around and, from the vantage point of being, take a look at human being. It should be emphasized that Heidegger's conception of his own philosophical enterprise contained this turning or shift or perspective from the very outset. After all, his lifelong question was the meaning or truth of being, but he had to start with human being as the only being who has access to being. Thus, one cannot say that he 'changed his mind'.

Many interpreters of Heidegger then sought a turning in his views, and there was a great deal of speculation as to just when this supposed turning took place.

However, as the guiding question of the first beginning gives way to the fundamental question of the other beginning, we are not talking about some kind of turn in Heidegger's method (*methodos*), in his path of thought, but about a turning in being itself. The most common formulation of this turning is this:

In the turning of Appropriation the presencing of truth is the truth of presencing. And this oppositionality (*Widerwendigkeit*) itself belongs to being as such.[27]

In contrast to the either-or that we have been discussing, the turning seems to point to a both-and, and the two forces of this both-and are in strife. *Beiträge* was written at about the time of the essay

"The Origin of the Work of Art." In that essay, Heidegger was very much preoccupied with the strife between world and earth. *Beiträge* continues to develop the basic thought, going somewhat beyond it, yet less developed and clearly worked out. One can see the development of the Fourfold in the making. The strife oscillates between *Da-sein* and Appropriation, being and beings, being and nonbeing, presence and absence, belongingness and call or neediness. Another term for strife is 'the Between'. The 'not' plays an expanded role in most of these formulations.

A, *the* turning which indicates the presencing of being itself as the Appropriation countervibrating within itself.
    The Appropriation grounds within itself *Da-sein* (I). *Da-sein* grounds the Appropriation (II). Grounding is here obverse (*Kehrig*): I. bearing and towering through, II. establishing (*stiftend*) and projecting.[28]

The Appropriation bears and towers through *Da-sein. Da-sein* makes room for and establishes the Appropriation. In this formulation strife is downplayed; the emphasis is more on mutual support.
    As in *Identity and Difference*, Heidegger is not thinking two things that are related, but rather a nonsubstantial relation that first generates what is related. The unusual, nonmetaphysical, poetic terms attempting to express this nonsubstantial relation are, for example, 'vibration' (*Schwingung*) and 'betrembling' (*Erzitterung*).

Presencing is not supposed to name something that again lies *beyond* being, but rather what expresses what is innermost about it, Appropriation, that countervibration of being and *Da-sein* in which both are not objectively present poles, but pure vibration itself.[29]

To simplify things, one could perhaps say that the turning and the between present a general, neutral structure within which, then, being and nothing, Appropriation and *Da-sein,* or the gods and man can encounter each other.

What here enters into the there is inmost concealment, the reciprocal relation of the there to the away turning toward it, is the reflection (*Widerschein*) of the turning in the presencing of

being itself. The more primordially being is experienced in its
truth, the deeper the *nothing* is as the abyss on the edge of the
ground.[30]

"Away" (*weg*) here refers to *Da-sein* when it is not really *da*,
there, what Heidegger terms the more primordial word for the inauthenticity of *Da-sein*. Again, Heidegger is attempting to think the
play of presence and absence other than as a mutually exclusive
conflict between objective presence and nugatory nothingness, between eternalism and nihilism.

The Appropriation in its turning is neither exclusively contained in the call nor in the belongingness, in neither of the
two and yet vibrating both, and the betrembling of this vibration (*das Erzittern dieser Erschwingung*) in the turning of the
Appropriation in the most concealed presencing of being. This
concealment needs the deepest clearing. Being 'needs' *Da-
sein*.[31]

"Vibrating" is used not adjectivally but as a transitive verb: vibrations produce sound, they vibrate sound. The same is true of "betrembling": the betrembling produces the vibrations. Heidegger is
here completely in the nonsubstantive realm of sound and movement, yet a movement not encompassed by the Aristotelian four
classifications of movement or change as quantitative, qualitative,
local motion, and coming into being and passing away. We are inclined to think movement almost exclusively as local motion, going
somewhere. But vibrating and, especially, trembling cannot be so
categorized; they are also neither mechanical nor teleological.

Being presences as the between for the god and man, but in
such a way that this between space first generates the essential possibility for the god and man, a between that overflows
its banks and first lets banks originate from the surf, ever belonging to the stream of the Appropriation, ever concealed in
the richness of its possibilities, ever the hither and yonder of
inexhaustible relations in whose clearing worlds constitute
themselves and decline, earths open themselves up and toler-
ate destruction.[32]

Here we have a definite prefiguration of the Fourfold, conceived as worlds, earths, man, and the god. Again there is the
thought that the surf of the between first generates its own banks.

Of course, our customary way of thinking is left with the question of what the between was between in order for it to be called "the between." If the banks were not there to being with, what was the between between? For the primordial relation that generates its own relata we can at least come up with an ontic example: marriage. A marriage first generates and defines a husband and wife. Before the marriage, there were, of course, a man and a woman but not a husband and a wife. Still, this example is ontic.

The recognition of man's belongingness to being through the god, the god's confession, which does not diminish him nor his greatness, that he needs being.
The belongingness to being and this needing of being first reveal being in its self-concealing as that oppositional (kehrige) center in which belongingness exceeds needing, and needing towers over belongingness: being as Ap-propriation that takes place out of the oppositional excess of itself and thus becomes the origin of the strife between the god and man, between the passing by of the god and the history of man.[33]

Being is the oppositional center in which man's belongingness to being and the god's need for being meet and strive against, or with, each other. The most mature formulation of this thought can be found in *Identity and Difference* where what is in question, however, is not man and the god but being and beings. However the individual components may vary, the structure, meeting in the oppositional center, is basically the same. This would support Heidegger's claim to think the relation before the relata. Since this text has been unavailable for some time, I quote at length.

Being here becomes present in the manner of a transition to beings. But being does not leave its own place and go over to beings, as though beings were first without Being and could be approached by Being subsequently. Being transits (that), comes unconcealingly over (that) which arrives as something of itself unconcealed only by that coming-over (Überkommnis). Arrival means: to keep concealed in unconcealedness—to abide present in this keeping—to be a being. Being shows itself as the unconcealing overwhelming. Beings as such appear in the manner of the arrival that keeps concealed in uncon- cealedness. Being in the sense of unconcealing overwhelming, and beings as such in the sense of arrival that keeps itself con- cealed, are present, and thus differentiated, by virtue of the

Same, the differentiation. That differentiation alone grants
and holds apart the 'between,' in which the overwhelming and
the arrival are held toward one another, are borne away from
and toward each other. The difference of Being and beings, as
the differentiation of overwhelming and arrival, is the perdurance (*Austrag*) of the two in *unconcealing keeping in concealment*. Within this perdurance there prevails a clearing of what
veils and closes itself off—and this its prevalence bestows the
being apart, and the being toward each other, of overwhelming
and arrival.[34]

With a final quote from *Beiträge* we take leave of the question
of the turning and move on to the rather enigmatic problem of instantaneity. This quote shows that the god is very much present in
these deliberations and that we cannot evade briefly addressing the
question of the god later on.

And in the turning: the Appropriation must need and use
Dasein, needing it, place it in the call and thus bring it before
the passing by of the last god.
  The turning presences between the call (to the belonging
ones) and the hearing (*Zugehör*) (of those called). Turning is
counter-turning. *The call* to the leap into Appropriating is the
greatest stillness of the most concealed self-knowing. . . .
  The Appropriation thus 'is' the highest dominance as the
counter-turning above approach and flight of the gods who
have been there. The most extreme god needs being.
  The *call* is onfall and remaining absent in the mystery of
Appropriating. In the turning the beckonings of the last god
are at play as the onfall and remaining absent of the arrival
and flight of the gods and their place of dominance.[35]

We now simply draw attention to the complexity of this passage, by no means an isolated instance. Both arrival and flight of
the gods can take place as well as remain absent. Arrival of the gods
can occur; flight of the gods can occur. Arrival of the gods can remain absent; flight of the gods can remain absent. There is no such
thing here as simple presence (eternalism) or simple absence (nihilism). A discussion of time and instantaneity can throw some light
on the question of presence and absence. We shall be unable to
present a developed position, as most of Heidegger's remarks on
this subject are exclusively in *Beiträge,* which does not develop its

topics in the manner of a lecture or an essay. Still, there is much that is suggestive and fruitful.

Instantaneity

As far as I can see, Heidegger's sparing remarks in *Beiträge* on instantaneity and the place of the moment (*Augenblicksstätte*) do not present a developed theory. They present consistent insights that, although themselves left undeveloped, invite cautious speculation—speculation, not in the sense of wild guesswork or grandiose systems, but in the root meaning of the term '*speculari*', to see, to have insight.

An absolutely key and crucial passage may serve to set our thinking in motion.

> Being—the remarkable false belief that being must always 'be,' the more constant and longer lasting, the more 'in being' it is. But first of all being 'is' not at all, but it presences. And then being is the most rare because the most unique and no one can figure the few moments in which it grounds a place for itself and presences.[36]

The first statement in this passage delivers a radical blow to the basic position of Western philosophy: What endures and is permanent is what is real; what does not, is not. What changes and is unable to persist and last simply is not real.

How can what changes be real? But Heidegger has asserted no such thing. He is simply saying that constancy and persistence not only are not the criteria for the real but do not exist at all in the way we imagine. What changes presupposes the continuity of an objectively present persisting substratum. From the time of *Being and Time* on, Heidegger has consistently and forcefully denied the existence of any such objectively present substratum. He also denies that the Greeks thought this kind of substratum.

> The *aei* of the Greeks is not the historiographically thought duration of progressive endless duration, but the constancy (*Beständigkeit*) of the presencing (*Anwesung*) of inexhaustible presence (*Wesen*).[37]

Although Heidegger is also critical of much of the first beginning with Greek philosophy, he is careful not to read later developments back into it. Thus, while he is highly critical of Aristotle's theory of time, with its emphasis on the *nun*, the now, as what is alone objectively present and real, he is not going to read the flattened down version of Christian 'eternity' back into the Greeks. And, especially in *Beiträge*, he is more and more critical of the Platonic *idea* as the universal (*koinon*) under whose yoke (*zugon*) all things, the soul included, fall.

In this context, we can probably learn more from Heidegger's polemic which *implies* a different conception of time than we can from his own, somewhat cryptic, 'positive' remarks.

> Thinking in the sense of re-presenting something in general and this as *making present* (*Gegenwärtigung*) and thus presenting the area in which beings are grasped in terms of constant presence, without the temporal character of this interpretation being recognized. That is so little the case that even after *ousia* was interpreted in *Being and Time* as constant presence and this presence was conceived in its temporal nature, people continued to talk about the *timelessness* of 'presence' and 'eternity,' for the reason that they held on to the common concept of time that only exists as a framework for what changes and thus can have no effect upon what is constantly present.[38]

Heidegger is here not only denying the possibility of timelessness, but also, by implication, attacking the conception of change taking place within the framework of time (time *in which*). There is no timelessness, nor is there its opposite, change in time, because there is no persisting substratum on which, or in which, continuous change could occur. The implication here is that time is in some sense *discontinuous*.

There are perhaps only five passages (I do not have a computer) in *Beiträge* where Heidegger uses the term 'instantaneity' (*Augenblicklichkeit*). He speaks more often of the moment or the place of the moment (*Augenblicksstätte*) as the concrete occurrence of instantaneity, its specific instance, instantiation, or occurrence. This is by no means to say that the moment or the place of the moment is a particular 'example' of a universal instantaneity.

A word about the English term 'instantaneity'. Heidegger has always referred to the "moment" (*Augenblick*). The German *Augenblick*, like the French *coup d'oeil,* is better captured by the somewhat cumbersome English phrase "the twinkling of an eye." The English *moment* does as well as anything, but when substantivized as *momentariness* it has the unavoidable, exclusive connotation of fleeting passing by, and thus of change in the traditional sense, which is precisely what Heidegger wants to rethink.

> When and how was the place of the moment for the truth of being ever thoughtfully asked about and its grounding prepared, thoroughly and bracketing all of the traditional current theories? . . . *Time-space* is to be developed in its presencing as the *place of the moment* of the Appropriation. However, the 'moment' is never just the tiny remainder of 'time' that can hardly be pulled together.[39]

'Instantaneity' seems to lack the exclusive connotation of fleetingness, of the tiny remainder of time, and, moreover, has a root connection (by accident?) with Heidegger's important conception of *Inständigkeit* (standing within, perdurance). The term 'instantaneity' seems to stress more the actual *taking place* of something and not just its fleetingness. These considerations are mostly intuitive; they may be somewhat arbitrary.

The three passages containing this term are:

> Being becomes what is strange (*das Befremdliche*) in such a way that the grounding of its truth increases the strangeness and thus holds all beings of *this* being in its (being's) strangeness. Only then does the complete uniqueness of the Appropriation and all the instantaneity of *Da-sein* allotted to that uniqueness fulfill itself.[40]

> *Being presences as the Appropriation.* There belongs to the Appropriation uniqueness and strangeness in the instantaneity of the place that took root in an unhoped for way and thus spread itself out.[41]

> The leap is a knowing leap into the instantaneity of the place of the onfall.[42]

Throughout *Beiträge*, Heidegger is very clear in emphasizing the uniqueness and strangeness of being. He totally rejects the traditional conception of being as the most universal concept and even the idea that being is something familiar. The 'preontological understanding of being' has very much receded into the background. Being is utterly unique and totally strange, even somewhat alienating. After all, what conceals itself and withdraws is hardly your garden-variety friendly next-door neighbor.

One would like to follow the customary conception of time since Plato and Aristotle and leave the *nun* its precedence, only deriving past and future from its transformation, especially since memory can only remember from and in the appeal to something present and something that has been present, since what is futural only has the determination to become something present.

Although what is present is never what is not and has a share in the grounding of memory and preparation, all of this only if the making present of what is present is already supported and attuned by memory and preparation from whose intimacy alone the present always flashes up (*aufblitzt*). Primordially experienced, the present cannot be calculated in terms of its fleetingness, but in terms of its *uniqueness*. Uniqueness is the new and essential content of the constancy and presencing from memory and preparation.[43]

Heidegger is talking not only about Plato and Aristotle in his discussion of the traditional concept of time, but here above all about Augustine, who stated that memory is the *present* recollection of the past and expectation is the *present* anticipation of the future. Whatever we experience of past or future we experience *in the present*. All three thinkers—Plato, Aristotle, and Augustine— are saying that what we experience, what is real, is the *present*.

There is a definite insight into time in these three thinkers, particularly Augustine. I cannot remember the past *in the past,* I cannot anticipate the future *in the future.* The present always plays a, or the, central role in what I experience. The crucial question is what kind of present that is: the 'knife-edged' now that is actually nothing but an abstraction, not an experience, or the fullness of a present that in a sense contains everything.

Heidegger, however, perhaps to avoid the conception of the knife-edged now, has always insisted on the togetherness of the three ecstasies (modes) of time. In the language of *Being and Time,* we project into the future; in so doing we come back to what has been, and the present is engendered. The primary ecstasy or mode of time is the future.

Although Heidegger later modifies his emphasis on the priority of the future somewhat, he never *radically* alters his original position, nor does he ever present any kind of modified, detailed description of temporality. However, what he was critical of in *Being and Time,* about the traditional concept of time, does become more clearly and unmistakably stated.

All metaphysics up to Hegel insists on always thinking time departing from the guiding interpretations of the being of beings. Thus, for example, Kant understands time in the horizon of ob-jectivity (*Gegen-ständlichkeit*) as what *constantly remains* in the continued flowing change of the nows.

In metaphysics, especially with Aristotle, there is thus a short circuit in the reflection on time in which is delineated what *Being and Time* calls the covering over of the meaning of being. This thinking must attempt to think a new—nonmetaphysical—manner of time, to get it underway, a manner that is not guided unawares by the ontological presupposition of the beingness of time, the effect of which on the metaphysical concept of time has the consequence that that concept is completely focussed on *what is present* (actually only what is present *is*; compared to what is present, past and future are conditioned by the lack of being, consequently they are *me onta*.)[44]

Heidegger wants to think *presencing,* not what is present. In the language of the *Es gibt* (there is), he wants to think the giving, not the gift. Therefore, he wants to get away from what is objectively present. We are not supposed to assume that what is real is *what is in being* and then look for that kind of thing in time. We are not supposed to look for a 'what' at all. Thus he expands and energizes the moment, the present, by thinking past and future as activities that not only enter into the present but actually *constitute* it, so that there is no such thing as a present devoid of past and future.

In what would the shift from temporality, so conceived, to something like instantaneity and the place of the moment, consist? Heidegger does not spell it out for us. But one thing is clear. The *continuity* essential to temporality is lacking in something like instantaneity and the place of the moment. We must try to pursue this as far as we can.

Its [necessity's] greatness consists in the fact that it needs no power and thus no violence and yet is more effective than these, although in the primordial manner of *its* own constancy (of the steadiness of the interrelated moments that seemingly has protracted interruptions.)[45]

Heidegger here thinks constancy as steadiness (*Stetigkeit*). Steadiness cannot be equated with duration and the changelessness that the philosophers have sought. Steadiness is a kind of continuous discontinuity, an inexhaustible occurring. "Continuous" points to inexhaustibility, "discontinuity" refers to the fact that occurring does not persist but happens again and again. Thought in this way, continuity and discontinuity almost coincide; we have here a temporal example of Cusanus's *coincidentia oppositorum.* In this case, it is not two things that coincide but the 'vertical' and 'horizontal' dimensions of occurrence.

Our calculative way of thinking immediately fastens on the phrase "seemingly protracted interruptions between the moments." We want to know *how long* between the moments. This misses the point of what is being said here.

> This historical moment is not an 'ideal state' because the moment goes against the essence of history each time, but this moment is the Appropriating of that turning in which the truth of being comes to the being of truth since the god needs being and man as *Da-sein* must have grounded the belongingness to being. Then, for this moment, being as the most intimate between is like the nothing, the god overpowers man and man exceeds the god, immediately, so to speak, and yet both only in the Appropriation which is the truth of being itself. But there will be a long history with many setbacks and much that is concealed before this incalculable moment that can never be as superficial as a 'goal.'[46]

This historical moment constitutes a sort of irruption in the course of history. In this moment being becomes, so to speak, transparent, like the nothing, and man and the god encounter each other in their belonging together. The moment cannot be calculated and it can never be an ideal state since it is in no sense a continuation of what went before.

> Even in the most supreme time only moments, uniqueness, not a state or a rule, not an ideal. . . .
> And what 'is' then (when the decision has been ventured). *Then* this question is impossible, then, for a moment, the Appropriation is event. This moment is *the time of being.*[47]

The lack of continuity in time is also expressed in words and phrases such as "the suddenness of a new epoch," "the leap," "the flashing up (*Aufblitzen, Erblitzen*) of being," "uniqueness" (no moment like any other, the moments are not homogeneous), "the push (*Stoss*) of being," and even in earlier expressions from *Being and*

Time such as "project" (*Entwurf*) and "thrownness" (*Geworfenheit*).
If I throw a ball (and the ball is thrown), everything is decided in
the moment in which I throw. The ball, of course, runs its course,
but direction and velocity are decided when I let go of it. The same
is true of the leap.

We turn now briefly to the question of the god before moving
back to our final question of concealment and finitude.

The God

The main question regarding the god or gods is, surprisingly
enough, not the obvious one asking whether we are speaking about
one god or many gods. We, in the Judeo-Christian tradition, are en-
tirely geared to monotheism—that is, not only one god numerically,
but one god exclusively and alone. Polytheism seems to us primitive
and mythological (as with the Greeks).

> The last god has his most unique uniqueness and stands out-
> side of every calculating determination intended by the labels
> 'mono-theism,' 'pan-theism' and 'a-theism.' 'Monotheism' and
> all kinds of 'theism' have existed only since Judeo-Christian
> 'apologetics' which has 'metaphysics' as its intellectual presup-
> position. All theisms become untenable with the death of this
> god. The multiplicity of god is not subject to number, but
> rather the inner wealth of grounds and abysses in the place of
> the moment of the gleaming apparition (*Aufleuchten*) and the
> concealment of the beckoning of the last god.
>   The last god is not the end, but the other beginning of im-
> measurable possibilities of our history.[48]

A great deal of theological discussion takes place within the
parameters of what Heidegger here rejects: monotheism (good),
pantheism (heresy), and atheism (anathema). The main phrase in
Beiträge, to which a section is devoted, is the passing by of the last
god. In the later formulation of the Fourfold we are dealing with the
godlike ones (*die Göttlichen*). Singularity or plurality is not so important here, because we are not talking about *beings* in the traditional, calculable sense of that word. In addition, Heidegger also
rejects the two attempts subsequent to the death of God to conceive
a higher being, Nietzsche's overman and Rilke's Angel.[49]

But the talk about the 'gods' does not mean here the decisive assertion of an objective presence of a plurality as opposed to a unique singularity, but refers to the undecidedness of the being of the gods, whether one or many. This undecidedness contains the questionability of whether something like being can be attributed to the gods without destroying everything godlike. The undecidedness as to what god and whether a god will once again become the most extreme need for what essence of man in what way, is named with the name 'the gods.'[50]

We know that whatever Heidegger means by "the god" and "the gods" cannot be a highest being (*summa ens*) or a cause of itself or of anything else (*causa sui*). We are no longer dealing with an omnipotent creator-god, which is about all that the concept of god has come to mean to most people.

We do know from *Beiträge* that the gods need *being* and that man as *Da-sein* must ground the belongingness to being. Why do the gods need being and what does it mean that they need being?

To deny being to 'the gods' just means that being is not 'above' the gods and the gods are not above being. But 'the gods' need being. This statement already thinks the essence 'of' being. 'The gods' need being not as something which is their own (*Eigentum*) in which they themselves take a stand. 'The gods' need being in order, through being which does not belong to them, to belong to themselves. Being is what is needed by the gods; it is their need, and the neediness (*Notschaft*) of being names its presencing, what is needed by 'the gods,' but never what can be caused and conditioned. . . . Seen from the perspective of the gods, the thinking of the history of being is determined as that thinking of being which grasps the abyss of the neediness of being as what is first, and never seeks the essence of being in what is godlike as what is supposedly most in being.[51]

The fact that the gods do not possess being means that neither is being beyond them nor they beyond being. The gods cannot be equated with Plato's Good (*agathon*) that is beyond being, nor with Plotinus's One that is beyond everything, nor with Eckhart's Godhead that is beyond God. Heidegger has come to reject any kind of transcendence or even any kind of rank or levels (*Stufung*) such as those found in the hypostases of Plotinus's emanation. The gods are not the *highest* kind of 'thing' (to avoid the word *being* for now); they

are a *different kind* of thing. They are not humans, not the earth or
heaven; they are a part of the Fourfold and they have a function.
There is ambiguity in Heidegger's formulations here where one
would have very much liked clarity. On the one hand, neediness is
primarily ascribed to the gods: they need being. On the other hand,
however, Heidegger also speaks of the neediness of being which
most likely can mean only that being needs its truth grounded in
Da-sein. But the most frequent emphasis is on the gods' neediness.
They need what they do not have in order to belong to themselves,
to be 'self-related'. What is unequivocally clear is that being has
nothing to do with causes or conditions of possibility. We shall return presently to the question of possibility.

Taking the key phrase "the passing by of the last god," we must
ask, What is "the *last* god" and what is his "*passing by*"?

The *last* god is not an end, but the beginning's vibrating within
itself and thus the highest form of refusal since everything
having to do with a beginning withdraws itself and only presences in towering over everything already encompassed as futural in it and delivering over to its determining force.

The end *is* only there where beings have torn themselves
loose from the truth of being and denied all questionability
and that means any distinction, in order to posture themselves
in the endless possibilities of what has thus been let loose in
endless time. The end is the interminable and-so-forth, from
which the ultimate (*das Letzte*) as what is most original has
long since and from the very outset withdrawn. The end never
sees itself, but believes itself to be the culmination and thus
will be least of all ready and prepared to expect or experience
the *ultimate*.[52]

The contrast here is between end as the supposed culmination
of a continuous process and ultimate or last as what is in itself most
extreme, perhaps somehow faintly reminiscent of Anselm's "than
which nothing greater can be thought" (*quo maius cogitari nihil
possit*), which *cannot* be equated with a highest being, because,
strictly speaking, it cannot become an object of thought. A highest
being is very definitely an object of thought. The end in this interpretation is comparable to what Keiji Nishitani termed "the infin-
itude of finitude," which, in its way, is somewhat akin to Hegel's
"bad infinity." The end is not an end at all, but the impotence of the
interminable and-so-forth that is *unable* to stop. In contrast, the
last or the ultimate as what is most extreme is what never gets

involved in the process in the first place. It keeps to itself (*an sich halten, epochē*). This corresponds to a passage in *On Time and Being* where Heidegger speaks of sending.

> The history of Being means the destiny of Being in whose sendings both the sending and the It which sends forth hold back with their self-manifestation. To hold back is, in Greek, *epochē*. Hence we speak of the epochs of the destiny of Being. *Epochē* does not mean here a span of time in occurrence, but rather the fundamental characteristic of sending, the actual holding-back of itself in favor of the discernibility of the gift, that is, of Being with regard to the grounding of beings.[53]

Now we must ask what "the *passing by* of the last god" might mean. First of all, it is clear that he can never be objectively present like a thing or a being. Nor is he totally absent. At some moment, a *kairos*, he passes by; he does not 'hang around'.

> Such things as passing by and event and history can never be thought as kinds of 'movements' because *movement* (even thought as *metabole*) is always related to the *on as ousia* in which relation *dunamis* and *energeia* and their later heirs also belong.[54]

We conceive movement exclusively against the background of substance or a substratum, like a storm pictured on a weather map moving horizontally from east to west. But the last god does not 'pass by' starting in Boston and ending up in Los Angeles. His passing by is not a local motion from one place to the other in the parameters of Newtonian space.

Self-concealment and hesitating self-denial, which belong intrinsically to being, are capable of potentiating themselves into refusal (*Verweigerung*), which is a special way of giving and sending that, among other things, might bring the god close.

> The greatest nearness of the last god occurs when the Appropriation as hesitating self-denial potentiates itself to *refusal*. This is something essentially other than mere *absence*. Refusal, as belonging to the Appropriation, can be experienced only from the more primordial essence of being as it gleams in the thinking of the other beginning.[55]

Since Heidegger never described the thinking of the other beginning in great detail but only indicated the necessity of a thinking other than representational, calculative thinking (*vorstellen*)—that is, *Besinnung* and *Andenken* (pondering and thinking toward)—he is also somewhat reticent in his discussions of refusal. But refusal does have a direct connection with the other beginning and the possibility of the last god.

Who would ever have the faintest idea that refusal is being's supreme giving, its initial presencing itself. It occurs as the withdrawal that draws into the stillness in which, in accordance with its essence, truth newly comes to the decision whether it can be grounded as the clearing for self-concealment. This self-concealment is the unconcealing of refusal, letting belong to what is strange in the other beginning.[56]

We leave the rest of this discussion of refusal for our final chapter on concealment and finitude. But we can at least say, at this point, that there is a special connection between refusal and the other beginning and the last god.

Refusal is the supreme nobility of giving and the fundamental trait of self-concealing *whose* revealedness constitutes the primordial essence of the truth of being. Only thus does being become estrangement itself, the stillness of the passing by of the last god.[57]

Heidegger does point in the direction of this thought in *Vier Seminare*, the thought that being can generate and 'come up with' a god.

But it is not just a matter of a reversal, but of a *counterthrust*, a countermovement of the first 'is' working upon the second 'is.' But what does this 'is' that has been thrust around mean? Meister Eckehart said: *Istic-heit* [isness]. Being is God, now understood speculatively, means: Being 'ises' (*istet*) God, i.e., being lets God be God. 'Is' speaks transitively and actively here. Developed being itself (as it is developed in Hegel's *Logic*) first makes possible (in a speculative counterthrust) being-God.[58]

The term 'speculative' is here meant in contrast to 'metaphysical'. It was Hegel's insight that subject and predicate in the speculative proposition do not remain inertly in their fixed positions but interact, work over and transform each other.

Concealment and Finitude

We now return to the central question of this study: the finitude of being. Thus far we have discovered that finitude is important and essential to Heidegger as opposed to the Judeo-Christian conception of (positive) infinity. In this, Heidegger remains true to his affinity with the Greeks for whom infinity and the lack of limits meant a lack of being, a kind of nothingness of which, as Nietzsche first stated, they had a horror. In addition to limits, finitude has profoundly to do with concealment, hesitating self-denial, and refusal: in short, the Not.

According to Heidegger, it is precisely the concealment that is an essential part of the process of truth, *a-letheia,* that the Greeks neglected to think. With his concept of *zugon* (yoke) Plato focussed on *aletheia* as the brightness and light in which beings are seen and perceived by a perceiver (*noein*). Brightness, or the light, is what yokes beings and perception. The understanding of being is restricted to what presents an outward appearance, an *idea.* This yoke between perception and what presents an *eidos* later becomes the relation between subject and object. Truth becomes correctness.

> Thus because *aletheia* becomes *phos* (light), the character of the *a-privativum* gets lost when interpreted in terms of light. The question of *concealment* and concealing, their provenance and their ground, does not arise. Because only what is 'positive' about nonconcealment, so to speak, the free access and what grants access is thematized, *aletheia* in this respect, too, loses its primordial depth and abysmal character.[59]

Perhaps nowhere else is Heidegger's analysis of the loss of *aletheia* so explicit as in *Beiträge.* For Plato, what was real was what could be seen, the *idea,* what presented an outward appearance and a shape for perception. The *idea* itself was conceived as something universal, accessible not to physical vision but only to the vision of the mind. The universal *idea* is then the 'cause' of all the individual beings and perception. Truth gets lost because there is no consideration of the *lethe* in *a-letheia,* but only of being accessible in brightness and light to perception. Herein lie the roots of the later development into subjectivity and objectivity. These conceptions are themselves foreign to the Greeks, but the germ had been planted. Being and concealment are lost.

> A-letheia means unconcealment and what is unconcealed itself. This already indicates that concealing itself is experienced only as what is to be removed, what must be taken away (a-). For this reason questioning does not go after concealing itself and its ground; thus what is revealed is also in turn alone essential; not unconcealing as the clearing in which concealing itself comes into the open. Thus concealing is not abrogated but first comprehensible in its essence.[60]

What is crucial for Heidegger is that we become aware of concealing, that concealing come into the clearing. We are not to think of concealing as inessential, unimportant, as something to be gotten rid of, as mere absence or negativity.

> As little as the open and openness were pursued in their presencing (the Greeks had a different task), the presencing of concealment-concealing was not clear and accessible to fundamental experience. Here, too, in a genuine Greek manner what was concealed became what was absent, and the occurrence of concealing was lost.[61]

Certainly in Beiträge, and almost everywhere else as well, concealing is so central to being that a synonym for being or Appropriation could read: "clearing of self-concealing." The question might arise as to what role concealing plays in Heidegger's other late name for being: the Fourfold. Since the Fourfold is not constituted by four related things or objects, concealing certainly is present in, above all, earth, but also in the godlike ones who, after all, flee and pass by, and in Da-sein itself which is often weg (away) and precisely not da (there). But there is no separate principle of concealment in the Fourfold. The persistent question remains whether the meaning of this concealment is sheltering (Bergung) or distortion and disessence (Unwesen). One would somehow like to say what belongs to being is sheltering, and the disessence is a kind of degeneration of that sheltering, but one cannot do that without distorting Heidegger.

> Whence does sheltering have its need and its necessity? From self-concealing. In order not to get rid of self-concealing, but rather to preserve it, the sheltering of this occurrence is needed.[62]

To restate what we have discovered thus far, what is most clear is what Heidegger *rejects:* any possible kind of infinity and any total revealing or unconcealing of being. Thus, the finitude of being consists in its 'hiding' from us even though it 'needs' us. This is where we remain if we strictly abide with what Heidegger said.

Our questioning throughout this study has attempted to discover conclusively whether finitude has a preserving function or a distorting one. We might hazard the suggestion that the history of being as metaphysics has indeed resulted in a kind of distortion, a distortion that has landed us in the era of the essence of technology. If the process of the history of being as metaphysics can be transmuted into Appropriation, into the belonging together of being and human being, then that process would be reabsorbed into the structure of being, and concealing would take on the indisputable meaning of saving and preserving.

The often-quoted words of Hölderlin seem to apply:

> But where there is danger, there grows
> also what saves.

Possibility: The Modalities

In the hope of throwing some light on this question from another perspective, we want to look into what Heidegger says about *possibility*. This may seem strange and far-fetched at first, but it may give us some additional insight into being, not conceived metaphysically as the ground and cause of being.

> Thinking *is*—this says: Being has fatefully embraced its essence. To embrace a 'thing' or a 'person' in its essence means to love it, to favor it. Thought in a more original way such favoring (*Mögen*) means to bestow essence as a gift. Such favoring is the proper essence of enabling, which not only can achieve this or that but also can let something essentially unfold in its provenance, that is, let it be. It is on the 'strength' of such enabling by favoring that something is properly able to be. This enabling is what is properly 'possible' (*das Mögliche*), that whose essence resides in favoring. From this favoring Being enables thinking. Being is the enabling-favoring, the 'may be' (*das Mög-liche*).[63]

Basically, Heidegger wants to rethink all of the modalities of being: reality, possibility, and necessity. His chief criticism is of the overwhelming emphasis on the *present* as what is exclusively real. What is real is what is objectively present. Future (possibility) and past are not real; future is *not* yet objectively present, the past is *no* longer objectively present. For Heidegger, it is the *future* which assumes a primary role—in *Being and Time,* as what is coming toward us (*Zukunft*) and is already presencing in the present moment. In "The Letter on Humanism" and elsewhere, the emphasis shifts subtly from the future to the modality of the possible. But the possible is not conceived in contrast to actuality, as *potentia* in contrast to *actus.* Rejecting the metaphysical scheme of potentiality–actuality and the related essence–existence, Heidegger takes the possible in an absolute sense, considered by itself and not in contrast to anything else. He goes one of his favorite routes, that of etymology. The root of the German word for "possible," *das Mögliche,* is the verb *mögen,* to like. The term *'Vermögen'*—faculty, ability, enabling—is also formed from this verb. Thus, Heidegger concentrates on the meaning of "liking" as the root of possibility and of any ability. What I like or am attracted to is in all probability something for which I have some ability, something that is possible for me. Conversely, what I do not like I am probably not going to be very good at. Thus, liking is the basis for ability and possibility. Heidegger has moved away from his Kantian emphasis, in *Being and Time,* on *conditions of possibility* to liking as what can help us to understand what possibility is and how it works.

This conception of possibility does not view it as the 'not yet' of actuality; possibility is not geared to actualization.

'Ground of possibility' is still *spoken* metaphysically, but is *thought* from the abysmal, perduring *belongingness.*[64]

Heidegger is here attempting to justify his occasional use of metaphysical terminology, particularly phrases such as "ground" and "conditions of possibility" that were indispensable to him in *Being and Time.* He gradually ceased coining new terms and began using some old and familiar terms in a new way.

The presencing of being will always remain closed to philosophy as long as it thinks one could know and, so to speak, construct being by cooking up various concepts of modality. Apart from the questionable origin of the modalities one thing is

decisive here: the leap into being as Appropriation; *only* from
here does the chasm (*Zerklüftung*) open itself.[65]

Modalities are ways to be. Heidegger rejects the three traditional ones and adopts the term 'the chasm' in their place. He states
that the chasm cannot be neatly ordered and classified in categories
or even structures. True to his conviction, he does not even attempt
to do this. Thus, "the chasm" pretty much turns out to be another
word for what he consistently describes as the between and the
turning.

The 'modalities' belong to beings (to beingness) and say nothing at all yet about the chasm of being itself. This can become
a question only if the truth of being as Appropriation makes
itself known (*aufleuchtet*), as what the god needs in that man
belongs to it. The modalities thus lag behind the chasm just as
beingness lags behind the truth of being; and the question of
the modalities is necessarily marooned in the framework of
the leading question, whereas the question of the chasm is
proper to the fundamental question alone. The chasm has its
first and broadest dimension (*Ausmessung*) in the need of the
god on the one hand and in the belongingness (to being) of man
on the other. The plunges of the god and the ascent of the man
grounded in *Da-sein* presence here. The chasm is the inner, in-
calculable turning out (*Ausfälligkeit*) of *Appropriating,* of the
presencing of being as the center that is needed and used and
grants belonging, that is at the same time related to the passing by of the god and the history of man.[66]

The chasm is a name for the center of the Fourfold, the between of the god and man, earth and world (heaven). "Chasm," "center," and "between" name something absolutely nonsubstantial, the
activity of the Not about which we can say only that it is in the center and not on the periphery of things. It *is* the center.

The provenance and dominance of the 'modalities' is *still* more
questionable than the interpretation of beings in terms of *idea*
as it took root in the course of the history of philosophy, becoming, so to speak, an objectively present 'problematic' in itself. For their provenance the precedence of 'reality' is
important (cf. also *existentia* as *the* distinction from *essentia*),
reality as *energeia,* possibility and necessity as its horns, so to
speak.[67]

In contrast to the preoccupation in the whole of Western philosophy, beginning with Plato's *eidos* and *idea* which seek to grasp reality as constant objective presence in the now, Heidegger wants to think, not presence, but *presencing*. At first glance the difference does not seem to be very great: same word, conceived now as a noun and then as a verb. But the difference is more far-reaching and has implications broader than merely a grammatical one. What is most important about presencing is not just that it is verbal; what is above all important is that presencing is *nonsubstantial;* it is not *ousia*. It is also not primarily geared to sight (*idea, eidos*). The goal of Heidegger's philosophical quest, the truth of being, is nonsubstantial.

The Western philosophical emphasis on reality and existence seeks to ascertain whether or not something is or is not. To ask about the existence or reality of something is simply to ask whether it is or is not. Arguments about the existence of God, for example, simply seek to prove that God exists or does not exist. Beyond that, the inquiry stops.

In contrast to the philosophical doctrine of the modalities, Heidegger wants to rethink the two of them that were never considered in their own right: possibility and necessity.

> The collision of necessity and possibility. Only in such realms can one guess what truly belongs to *that* which 'ontology' treats as the pale and empty *mish-mash* of the 'modalities.'[68]

Ontology divides what-is, beings, into the possible, the real, and the necessary—the modalities. For ontology, anything is logically possible that does not contradict itself. A pink elephant, to use the classic example for people 'seeing' something that does not exist, is possible even if no such animal actually exists. Someone could conceivably paint some poor elephant pink. Real is what is actually *there* for someone to ascertain. What is real is what happens to exist. What is necessary is what has to exist. Philosophical examples of what has to exist are pretty much exhausted by 'God' and 'mathematical truths', both of which have since come under critical scrutiny:

> Only in being does the *possible* presence as its deepest chasm so that being must first be thought in the thinking of the other beginning in the form of the possible. (But metaphysics makes the real as beings the point of departure and the goal of the determination of being). . . . That being is and thus does not

become a being is expressed most precisely as follows: being is possibility, what is never objectively present and yet always grants and denies in the refusal through ap-propriating.[69]

There is so much expressed and implied in *Beiträge* that one can more or less get lost in it. For this reason, we now simply leave *Beiträge* and turn to a few of the later writings. For our focus we shall choose a few key questions. But first, to conclude our discussion of possibility, we turn to *The End of Philosophy*. The context is a discussion of Leibniz in general and in particular of his "Twenty-four Statements."

Looking back to the traditional distinction of *potentia* and *actus,* the *vis* is characterized, so to speak, as the intermediate being between the two. In truth, this signifies overcoming the previous concepts of possibility and reality. The inquiry, however, is in the service of the improvement of 'first philosophy' which asks about the beingness of beings and acknowledges the *substantia* as what truly is. *Vis* is the name for the Being of self-contained beings. Accordingly, this Being consists neither in the *actualitas,* in that it means the production of what merely lies present, nor in the *potentia* in the sense of the predisposition of a thing for something (for example, of the tree trunk for a wooden beam). The *vis* has the character of *conatus,* of the already driving endeavor of a possibility. The *conatus* is in itself *nisus,* the inclination to realization. *Tendentia* thus belongs to *vis.*[70]

Leibniz thinks *tendentia,* tendency or inclination, as something belonging to being. We link this up with the passage quoted from "The Letter on Humanism" on liking and favoring and now try to inquire into what sort of 'activity' or 'stance' or 'attitude' is expressed in inclination and liking. Obviously a kind of *attraction.* If we may so ask for a moment, why is it that being is attracted? As something which is never objectively present, being nevertheless is not just nothing, not just the total absence of any presence whatsoever. One might venture to say that being is the *possibility* of presencing. This might be Heidegger's understanding of the "modality" of possibility; a liking for, an inclination to, presencing. This is not 'potentiality', not a germ that develops and comes to presence. Being as inclination and liking presences incalculably and freely in occasions, in historic deeds, great poets and writers, works of art. Being presencing in works of art is the only one of such occasions that Heidegger worked out, in the superb essay "The Origin of the Work of Art." There, Heidegger delineates how being, or the Fourfold, comes to presence in Van Gogh's painting of a pair of peasant woman's shoes. We see, not just a pair of shoes, but the *world* of the woman who wears them, her work in the fields, events of her life, and so on. Since, for Heidegger, being is never the most universal genus subsuming all particulars, it *presences* in a unique particular, totally. This cannot be thought as transcendent being becoming *immanent*. Heidegger completely relinquished his claim, in *Being and Time*, that being was the *transcendence par excellence*. Being is not objectively present 'anywhere' until and unless its presences. The insistent question of where it is when it is not presencing is inappropriate and simply has no answer. That is part of the mystery (*Geheimnis*) of being. However, strictly speaking, being does not become immanent either, since it does not remain (*manere*, to remain) anywhere. Being simply cannot be objectified.

By way of moving toward some sort of conclusion, we want to scrutinize, once again, Heidegger's two late names for being—"Appropriation" and the "Fourfold"—and finally to ask what happens to the question of concealment and finitude in these names. The use of the word *name* is intentional. Strictly speaking, neither Appropriation nor the Fourfold is a concept in the sense that some*thing* is grasped in or by them. First of all, they are not things but 'relations.' (For example, the Fourfold is not a thing; it presences *in* the thing.) Secondly, both "Appropriation" and the "Fourfold" are poetic names pointing to what they name; they are not logical concepts that could be fitted into the Aristotelian categories. Viewed grammatically, they are indeed nouns (or verbs, as in *Appropriating*), but nouns naming interrelationships.

To begin with a somewhat traditional remark, Appropriation, the belonging together of man and being, leaves out nature. This can remind us of Schelling's criticism of Hegel: Whereas Hegel ranks philosophy over art because philosophy attained the level of the pure concept unadulterated by anything physical or material. Schelling reversed this ranking, placing art above philosophy precisely because it *included* nature, not just as superseded (*aufgehoben*), but actual nature in its own independent right. Because of his overestimation of the concept and of language in general, Hegel failed to see the possibility that art can convey things that language alone cannot.

We begin with a consideration of Appropriation, which, after all, was Heidegger's predominant choice for a nonmetaphysical word for being, as is most apparent in *Beiträge* and in *Identity and Difference*. In contrast to the Fourfold, which appears to have no negative counterpart, Appropriation has not one but two counterparts: Framing and Expropriation. Here again we encounter the same ambiguity that we find in *Austrag* (perdurance): *Austrag* sometimes appears as a *process*, sometimes as a *structure*. Actually, the English translation of *Austrag* as perdurance better expresses the structural factor; it is perhaps less adequate to express the processual factor.

On the one hand, *Austrag* is conceived primarily as a process.

> By thinging, things carry out (*austragen*) world. Our old language calls such carrying *bern, bären*— Old High German *beran,* to carry, gestate, give birth, and *Gebärde,* bearing, gesture. Thinging, things are things. Thinging, they gesture—gestate—world.[1]

On the other hand, *Austrag* is conceived primarily as a structure.

> The perdurance (*Austrag*) of that which grounds and that which is grounded, as such, not only holds the two apart, it holds them facing each other. What is held apart is held in the tension of perdurance in such a way that not only does Being ground beings as their ground, but beings in their turn ground, cause Being in their way.[2]

Part of the problem and the ambiguity lies in our habitual tendency to think of a process as something going on and developing in the course of 'inauthentic' temporality, time conceived as a series of nows. This kind of time was critically discussed in *Being and Time.* What I am trying to intimate is that for another kind of thinking—the nonrepresentational, noncalculative thinking of the other beginning—'process' might not be restricted to a serial course of events, and 'structure' might not be limited to a static constituency having nothing to do with time.

Some evidence of this problem is also present in the term '*Ereignis*'. *Ereignis* is a perfectly regular word in German for 'event'; yet it cannot be thought as an event *in* the course of serial time, since it is the *source* of any kind of time as well as of everything else.[3] The root *eigen* (own) has far more to do with what Heidegger is getting at than the word *event.*

The problem or ambiguity resurfaces with Appropriation, but with the added complexity that it is not only with Appropriation itself, but with its *counterpart,* that the question of process versus structure arises. We can sum up this question succinctly, perhaps too succinctly to be intelligible at first, as follows: If the counterpart to Appropriation is Framing, we are speaking about a potential process; if the counterpart is Expropriation, we are speaking about a structure, the full structure of Appropriation itself. From what we can gather from Heidegger's statements, Framing is something which may disappear and give way to Appropriation; Expropriation is something that belongs indissolubly to Appropriation. The *meaning* of these two counterparts embodies the one question of this study: Does concealment or finitude have the function of distortion or of sheltering and protecting? In the case of distortion, we are dealing with Framing, which may or may not give way to Appropriation. In the case of sheltering, we are dealing with Expropriation, which has a clearly preserving function. Nowhere does Heidegger state unequivocally that these two counterparts mutually exclude each other. But the late formulations do finally polarize these possibilities of distortion or preservation in a more distinct way than we have been able to find thus far.

We begin with Framing.

What we experience in the frame as the constellation of Being and man through the modern world of technology is a prelude to what is called the event of appropriation. This event, however, does not necessarily persist in its prelude. For in the event of appropriation the possibility arises that it may overcome the mere dominance of the frame to turn it into a more original appropriating. Such a transformation of the frame into the event of appropriation, by virtue of that event, would bring the appropriate recovery—appropriate, hence never to be produced by man alone—of the world of technology from its dominance back to servitude in the realm by which man reaches more truly into the event of appropriation.[4]

Here, the possibility is clearly stated that Framing may be replaced by Appropriation: the belonging *together* of man and being may be replaced by their *belonging* together. By emphasizing the belonging rather than the together, Heidegger wishes to indicate a more primordial relation between man and being, not determined by the categories, mediations, connections, and objectifications of metaphysics. But Heidegger offers no guarantee whatsoever that this will come about. We may get stuck 'permanently' in the Framing of modern technology. We simply do not know.

However, if we do not get stuck in Framing and if the *belonging* together of man and being should come about in an appropriate way, in the way of Appropriation, Heidegger has some intriguing conjectures as to what that might entail.

Between the epochal transformations of Being and its withdrawal, a relation can be seen which, however, is not a causal
relation. One can say that the further one moves away from
the beginning of Western thinking, from *aletheia,* the further
aletheia goes into oblivion; the clearer knowledge, consciousness, comes to the foreground, and Being thus withdraws itself. In addition, this withdrawal of Being remains concealed.
In the *kryptesthai* of Heraclitus, that withdrawal is expressed
for the first and last time. (*Physis kryptesthai philei.* Nature
loves to hide.) The withdrawal of *aletheia* as *aletheia* releases
the transformation of Being from *energeia* to *actualitas,* etc.
We sharply distinguish from this meaning of transformation
which refers to metaphysics, the meaning which is intended
when we say that Being is transformed—to Appropriation.
Here it is not a matter of manifestation of Being comparable to
the metaphysical formations of Being and following them as a
new manifestation. Rather, we mean that Being—together
with its epochal revelations—is retained in destiny. Between
the epochal formations of Being and the transformation of Being into Appropriation stands Framing. Framing is an inbetween stage, so to speak. It offers a double aspect, one might
say, a Janus head. It can be understood as a kind of continuation of the will to will, thus an extreme formation of Being. At
the same time, however, it is a first form of Appropriation
itself.[5]

The possible transformation of the present form of being,
Framing, into Appropriation cannot be compared to the transformation within metaphysics as the history of being. This possible
transformation is not yet another, new manifestation of being following upon all the other various epochs. Rather, being, together
with its epochal manifestations contained in destining, would, so to
speak, be reabsorbed into Appropriation. Between these two mutually exclusive possibilities, the series of epochs of being in the history of metaphysics and the reabsorption of being in Appropriation,
stands Framing, a Janus head whose one countenance looks toward
the epochs of being in metaphysics and the other toward the transformation of being into Appropriation. Framing is, at the same
time, the extreme development of technology and a preliminary intimation of Appropriation.

The remark in *Vier Seminare* that Framing is the photographic negative of Appropriation[6] is at best intriguingly suggestive. However, Heidegger is also more explicit when he states that

Appropriation cannot be thought with the help of the concepts of being and the history of being. His remarks here culminate in the following statement:

> There is no destined (*geschickliche*) epoch of Appropriation. Destining comes from Appropriating.[7]

This means that Appropriation cannot be destined or sent, since it is the source of all destining and sending. What was destined or sent in the history of being as metaphysics was *presence* (*Anwesenheit*), presence in different epochs as *idea, energia, actualitas,* and so on. Appropriation is not an epoch in the history of being; it is itself *epochē*. We have here again the ambiguity of a process and a structure. Appropriation cannot be dispersed into a process of epochs; it remains a structure, an *epochē* which has nothing to do with process.

This kind of *epochē* figures in a passage in *Vier Seminare* on letting as compared with giving and sending. A consideration of this discussion will conclude our remarks on Appropriation in relation to Framing. Heidegger returns here to his distinction of ontic–ontological that played a decisive role in *Being and Time*. In this particular passage, "ontic" pretty much takes on the meaning of metaphysical statements about being, whereas "ontological" now refers to the history of being, Heidegger's transitional alternative to ontology.

> 1) One is tempted to understand 'it gives' as 'it lets presence.' And the giving in 'it gives' is interpreted ontically through the emphasis on letting-presence. Thus when I say in French: there are (*es gibt*) trout in this brook, the 'il y a' is understood with regard to the presence of beings, to their presencing— and the 'letting presence' is understood bordering on 'making presence.' Heard in this way the 'it gives' is grasped ontically so that the emphasis is on the fact of being.
>
> 2) If the 'it gives' is thought with regard to an interpretation of letting itself, then the emphasis changes.
>
> Presence is no longer emphasized, but *letting* itself. 'It gives' then has the precise meaning of '*letting* presence.' Now it is no longer presence which captures our attention, but that on whose basis presence becomes independent by covering it over—letting itself, the gift of 'giving' that gives only its gifts, but conceals and withdraws itself in such giving.[8]

Now it is no longer a matter of ascertaining the fact of existence or nonexistence but of seeing what gives and allows existence, how existence comes to be. Even the verbal expression "presencing" is not sufficient to establish what Heidegger is getting at; we have to penetrate to what allows presencing to come about. That is the *epochē* of being.

One of the chief things that restricts "letting presence" to an ontic interpretation is understanding it in the sense of *"making presence."* Making pushes the whole matter being discussed here in the direction of the will to will, machination, the essence of technology. *Epochē*, keeping to oneself, cannot make or force anything.

In summary we can say that 'letting be' can be emphasized with three different significations.

The first points to what is (to beings). In contrast to the first signification the second would pay less attention to *what* there is, it gives (what is), than to *presencing* itself. Then we have an interpretation of being in the way that metaphysics gives it. But deep within the second emphasis lies the third where the emphasis is decidedly on *letting* itself that *allows* presencing. Since it allows (releases?) presencing, that is, since it lets being be, this third emphasis points to the *epochē* of being. In this third signification we are face to face with being *as* being and no longer with one of the forms of its destiny.

When the emphasis is on *letting* presencing be, there is not even room for the name being. *Letting* is then pure *giving* which itself points back to the It that gives which is understood as Appropriation.[9]

It is the *epochē* of being that lets presencing come about. This is not Husserl's *epochē,* the bracketing of the world in order to gain an unsullied view of pure consciousness. Nor is *epochē* epoch, one of the forms destined in the history of being. *Epochē* is keeping to itself. Only in keeping to itself, in concealing, withdrawing itself, can being let a clearing come about in which beings can be. Only by withholding its own presencing can being allow other beings to presence, can it let beings be. To use a favorite device of Heidegger's, in the recurrent phrase "clearing of self-concealment," self-concealment is not necessarily a *genitivus objectivus,* it is not what is revealed. Self-concealment is a *genitivus subjectivus;* it is what lets the clearing be. The *epochē* and self-concealment of being is what lets anything at all be, what makes room for things.

On the other hand, there is undeniably a negative, withdrawing, concealing element in being itself which will not give way, in any kind of process, to anything, since it is a structural constituent of being.

The self-withholding factor in being is, for example, what differentiates the present (*Gegenwart, Anwesenheit*) from the now (*Jetzt*). The now as conceived by Aristotle is, according to Heidegger, a now-point lacking dimensionality. In contrast, the dimensionality of the present, as opposed to the dimensionlessness of the now, is made possible by the fact that what has-been and what comes toward us do not themselves literally become present. If past and future became literally present, one could no longer speak of them as past and future and would land back in the Aristotelian now.

We note that absence, too, manifests itself as a mode of presence. What has-been which, by refusing the present, lets that become present which is no longer present, and the coming toward us of what is to come which, by withholding the present, lets that be present which is not yet present—both made manifest the manner of an extending opening up which gives all presencing into the open.[10]

If I examine my own experience and recall something that happened yesterday or anticipate something that will come about tomorrow, I could be intensely focussed on something not literally present but nevertheless very much *there*. And this, for Heidegger— it cannot be emphasized strongly enough—is not a matter of any kind of representation or picturing.

> Heidegger clarifies this by saying: when I think back in remembering René Char in Les Busclets, who or what is thereby given to me? René Char himself! God knows, not some kind of 'picture' through which I would be mediately related to him.[11]

This is a fascinating and extremely difficult question that we shall not pursue here. It involves the 'presence' of what is not physically, literally present, culminating in the problem of the transcendental imagination. (The English *image-ination* speaks less forcefully than the German *Einbildungskraft,* literally the power to instill or inculcate, a picture.) It is a problem which intrigued both Kant and Heidegger and on which they both got stranded.

Heidegger has moved from an emphasis on ground and grounding, still very much present in *Beiträge* (where the abyss was also present, often making it difficult to maintain the distinction, as in phrases such as "abysmal ground"), to the activities of giving and sending and, finally, of letting. Just as the abyss pointed to a kind of 'not' in grounding, giving and sending are "made possible" (it is difficult to avoid completely the Kantian phrase) by this dimension that is the main subject of our inquiry: self-withdrawal, self-refusal, *epoche*. That which does the sending or giving of epochs in the history of being does not send or give *itself* but only its destiny or gift. In fact, Heidegger defines sending as a giving that gives only its gift but holds itself back and withdraws.

In a passage near the end of the lecture "Time and Being," Heidegger finally mentions the various formulations of this dimension of the not, only to state that a discussion of them is not the subject of that lecture.

Along the way we have already thought more about it, although it was not explicit said: namely, that to giving as sending there belongs keeping back—such that the denial of the present and the withholding of the present, play within the giving of what has-been and what will be. What we have mentioned just now—keeping back, denial, withholding—show something like a self-withdrawing, something we might call for short: withdrawal. But inasmuch as the modes of giving that are determined by withdrawal—sending and extending—lie in Appropriation, withdrawal must belong to what is peculiar to the Appropriation. This, however, no longer belongs to the matter of this lecture.[12]

However, in the published version there follow, in brackets, several paragraphs that were presumably not communicated at the time of the lecture. We cite the most important core of these remarks.

[In true time and its time-space, the giving of what has-been, that is, of what is no longer present, the denial of the present manifested itself. In the giving of the future, that is, what is not yet present, the withholding of the present manifested itself. Denial and withholding exhibit the same trait as self-withholding in sending: namely, self-withdrawal.

Insofar as the destiny of Being lies in the extending of time, and time, together with Being, lies in Appropriation, Appropriating makes manifest its peculiar property, that Appropriation withdraws what is most fully its own from boundless unconcealment. Thought in terms of Appropriating, this means: in that sense it expropriates itself of itself. Expropriation belongs to Appropriation as such. By this expropriation, Appropriation does not abandon itself—rather, it preserves what is its own.][13]

Here we finally have a clear statement as to the function of the not: withdrawal, withholding, denial, keeping to itself, concealment. All of this *preserves* Appropriation. There is no trace of distortion here. Since it is a late statement and presumably shows Heidegger's most mature stance in this matter, we must take it seriously. And yet we cannot simply ignore the statements describing distortion.

We turn now to the Fourfold. Whereas Appropriation was still a formulation of the fundamental philosophical question of identity (albeit somewhat idiosyncratic), the Fourfold is clearly a formulation that is poetic. It is here that Heidegger brings in 'nature', the earth and the heaven, and also the godlike ones. Man as the mortal has been with us since *Being and Time*.

Earth is the building bearer, nourishing with its fruits, tending water and rock, plant and animal.

When we say earth, we are already thinking of the other three along with it by way of the simple oneness of the four.

The sky is the sun's path, the course of the moon, the glitter of the stars, the year's seasons, the light and dusk of the day, the gloom and flow of night, the clemency and inclemency of the weather, the drifting clouds and the blue depth of the ether.

When we say sky, we are already thinking of the other three along with it by way of the simple oneness of the four.

The divinities are the beckoning messengers of the godhead. Out of the hidden sway of the godhead the god emerges as what he is, which removes him from any comparison with beings that are present.

When we speak of the divinities, we are already thinking of the other three by way of the simple oneness of the four.

The mortals are human beings. They are called mortals because they can die. To die means to be capable of death as death. Only man dies. The animal perishes. It has death neither ahead of itself nor behind it. Death is the shrine of Nothing, that is, of that which in every respect is never something that merely exists, but which nevertheless presences, even as the mystery of Being itself. As the shrine of Nothing, death harbors within itself the presencing of Being. As the shrine of Nothing, death is the shelter of Being.[14]

For our purposes, we do not wish so much to dwell on the four elements of the Fourfold as to see how the Fourfold presences. The how of the Fourfold's presencing is the mirror-play.

Here again we have a twofold 'not' in relation to the Fourfold. The first not is clear and was discussed in the context of Appropriation. Where Framing and machination are perpetrated, the Fourfold cannot presence. There are, then, no *things* in the sense of that word that Heidegger develops in the essay "The Thing." Without the thing, the Fourfold is denied a site or location. Heidegger gives many examples of the impossibility of a location for the presencing, the mirror-play of the Fourfold, above all in "The Question Concerning Technology." There the hydroelectric plant is set into the current of the Rhine river, making the river a water-power supplier. This river is challenged to unlock, transform, and store up the energy concealed in it. Nothing can presence here. The energy stored up is being distributed, regulated, and secured. The energy thus stored up constitutes what Heidegger calls the standing-reserve (*Bestand*). There is no possibility of a clearing in this situation. The path for the Fourfold to presence is simply blocked.

But there is a kind of not in the presencing of the Fourfold itself, comparable in a way to expropriation in Appropriation, that allows its activity as mirror-play. Mirror-play is a poetic name that excludes any kind of grounding or causality. The unity of the Fourfold is the source of the four, but nothing *causes* anything else. The term 'play' already excludes such modes of explanation. If Heidegger's reflections on identity grew out of Parmenides' statement that being and thinking belong together, his reflections on mirror-play have some roots in Heraclitus's fragment about Aion, the world power, being a child playing a game.

What about 'mirror'? This is where the not makes its appearance. Heidegger states that this mirroring does not portray a likeness, an image. Mirroring clears (*lichtet*) each of the four, thus appropriating the presencing of each of the four into belonging with one another. The nature of a mirror is such that anything can be reflected in it because it itself has no appearance within itself. The mirror is nothing but the possibility of mirroring and reflecting. If it were itself something, nothing could appear in it. But what appears in the mirror is not physically, literally in the mirror. Because the mirror is empty, nonsubstantial, it can receive the cleared 'things' in it which, in this mode of appearing, are also empty, nonsubstantial. Otherwise interpenetration is impossible. In order for earth and heaven, godlike ones and mortals to interpenetrate in the mirror-play, everything, including the mirroring, must be empty and nonsubstantial. The mirroring *clears* (i.e., empties) each of the four of their insistent self-nature.

The mirroring that binds into freedom is the play that betroths each of the four to each through the enfolding clasp (*Halt*) of their mutual appropriation. None of the four insists on its own separate particularity. Rather, each is expropriated, within their mutual appropriation, into its own being. This expropriative appropriating is the mirror-play of the fourfold.[15]

Appropriation, the *belonging* together of man and being, and the appropriating mirror-play of the Fourfold are possible only because nothing is objectively, substantially present. To say that each of the four is expropriated means that each is released, set free from insistence on its own particularity. Otherwise, nothing can belong together or join in the mirror-play of the Fourfold.

In the history of language, the German word 'opening' is a borrowed translation of the French *clairière*. It is formed in accordance with the older words *Waldung* (foresting) and *Feldung* (fielding). The forest clearing (opening) is experienced in contrast to dense forest, called 'density' (*Dickung*) in older language. The substantive 'opening' goes back to the verb 'to open.' The adjective *licht*, 'open,' is the same word as 'light.' To open something means: to make something light, free and open, e.g., to make the forest free of trees at one place. The openness thus originating is the clearing. What is light in the sense of being free and open has nothing in common with the adjective 'light,' meaning 'bright'—neither linguistically nor factually.[16]

Here we have good textual evidence for *Lichtung*, not as lighting, but close to lighte*n*ing. My translator's footnote to this reads, "Both meanings exist in English for light. The meaning Heidegger intends is related to lever (i.e., allieviate, lighten the burden)." I now would definitely prefer 'clearing' (which is, after all, the exact translation of the French word *clairière*, from which *Lichtung* comes) to 'opening', simply because Heidegger talks so much about the Open (*das Offene*) and thus the two terms, the 'Open' and the 'Opening', tend to get conflated in English.

The point of all this is that *Lichtung,* clearing, is very close to
the meaning of 'emptying.' It has nothing to do with light as lighting, which, together with darkness, is possible only when there is a
clearing. A clearing in the forest is apt to be lighter than the
thicket, but without the clearing, no light *or* darkness. Heidegger
definitely wants to get away from the emphasis on the visibility of
the *eidos.* Revealing and unconcealment are possible, not because
of *light,* but because of *clearing,* emptiness. This is a long way off
from Plato.

To play briefly and inconclusively with Heidegger's own favorite device, let us take the phrase as a Leitmotif: *Lichtung des Sich-
verbergenden* (clearing of self-concealing). We tend, I believe, to take
the genitive in self-concealing as a *genitivus objectivus,* an objective
genitive. Self-concealing is what is cleared. But if we consider for a
moment the possibility of its being a *genitivus subjectivus,* a subjective genitive, self-concealing becomes that which 'does' the clearing
and emptying. But, of course, as Heidegger says in *Beiträge,*[17] he
means a genitive *ureigener Art,* of its own primordial kind. The
Cartesian-based device of subjective and objective genitives can
shake up our thinking but is unable to provide any kind of ultimate help.

*   *   *

In conclusion, we return to our question of the finitude of being. We want to take a look at three of Heidegger's later statements
on finitude, and then see what we can make of the whole question of
finitude and concealment. Heidegger's own remarks on finitude are
clear and consistent.

The finitude of Being was first spoken of in the book on Kant.
The finitude of Appropriation, of Being, of the Fourfold hinted
at during the seminar is nevertheless different from the finitude spoken of in the book on Kant, in that it is no longer
thought in terms of the relation to the infinite, but rather is
finitude in itself: finitude, end, limit, one's own—to be secure
in one's own. The new concept of finitude is thought in this
manner—that is, in terms of Appropriation itself, in terms of
the concept of one's own.[18]

Heidegger wants to think a finitude that is beyond the quantitatively thought opposition of finite-infinite. One could interpret

the emphasis on Appropriation and one's own, particularly the phrase "secure in one's own," to mean free of Framing and the essence of technology. In that case, 'finite' would be brought close to the meaning of 'pure', unmixed with anything foreign.

However, what is absolutely clear is that Heidegger wants to distance himself from Hegel and from the whole tradition of Christianity with their emphasis on the Infinite as the really Real.

> If being needs man in this manner in order to be, a *finitude of being* must be assumed accordingly; that being is not thus absolutely for itself is in sharpest contrast to Hegel. For when Hegel says that the Absolute is not 'without us,' he says it only with respect to the Christian 'God needs man.' In contrast, for Heidegger's thinking being is not without its relation to *Dasein*.[19]

As we know by now, Heidegger decisively rejects *any* kind of infinity, be it that of the Christian God or even Rilke's Open. Limit, end, finitude must be, but ultimately not the limit or *peras* of Plato's *idea* or *eidos*. This limit, end, finitude must be thought from within. In this last passage, and in the one we are about to quote, we have one clear directive as to how this inner finitude must be thought: The *abysmal* character of being needs *Da-sein*, not just for being to reveal itself, but for being to 'be', that is, to presence. Being is Appropriation, the belonging together of being and man. Being is the Fourfolding, the worlding of world in which earth, heaven, the godlike ones, and the mortals presence. Being is nothing by itself. It is no-thing.

The Presencing of Being
(its finitude)

What does it mean: being 'is' in-finite? The question cannot be answered unless the presencing of being is not also in question. And the same thing is true of the statement: being is finite if in-finitude and finitude are taken as objectively present concepts of quantity. Or do they mean a *quality*, and which one?

The question of the presencing of being finally lies beyond the strife between those statements; and the statement being is finite is intended only as a transitional rejection of any kind of 'Idealism.' But if one moves within the strife of these statements, we should say: If being is posited as infinite, then it is precisely *definite* (*bestimmt*). If it is posited as finite, then its a-bysmalness is affirmed. For the in-finite cannot be thought as what is endless, flowing past and only running out, but as the closed *circle*. Appropriation, on the other hand, stands in its 'turning' (*Kehre*)! (strifeful).[20]

Speaking within the parameters of finite–infinite, Heidegger can say that if being is thought as in-finite, it must be thought as a *definite* infinity. If it is thought as finite, its abysmal character is brought out. This is all in accord with what we have been able to establish thus far: Being is not indefinite, "the night in which all cows are black," and it is abysmal in that it is not absolute; it needs *Da-sein*.

But being ap-propriates *Da-sein* to itself for the grounding of its truth, i.e., its clearing because without this clearing de-cision of itself into the neediness of the god and the guardian-ship of *Da-sein* it would have to consume itself in the fire of its own undissipated heat.
      How can we know how often this has already happened? If we knew it, we would not have the necessity of thinking be-ing in the uniqueness of its presencing.[21]

The latter statement is an intriguing, isolated remark. Heidegger seems to entertain briefly the possibility of multiple world conflagrations only to reject it in favor of the uniqueness of being. What prevents being from consuming itself in its own fire is its separation into the neediness of the god and the guardianship of man. The god needs being and being needs man.
      Ultimately, the 'appropriate' meaning of the finitude of being would appear to lie in its preserving and sheltering capacity. If the basic meaning of finitude is the lack of absoluteness, the need for man, and also the being-needed by the gods, that need finds its possible fulfillment in *Da-sein,* in man as the shepherd of being. In try-ing to establish a degree of clarity with regard to the question of concealment, a clarity not to be found in Heidegger, yet not incon-sistent with the main drift of his remarks, we may state that con-cealment and the not belong absolutely to being. The not and the concealment in the truth of being are what keeps being from being represented metaphysically as a being. It is always clear what Heidegger does *not* want to say; what he ultimately wants to say is not so simple (assuredly not for him either). But if concealment be-

longs *essentially* to being, it is not so clear whether, or in what way, something like abandonment—and, beyond that, even forgotten-ness—belongs to being.

But one thing is not only clear but also important. That is the meaning of finitude. Generally, we take finitude to mean that something is limited in time and space. We have already stated that the finitude thought by Heidegger is beyond the ordinary antithesis of finitude and infinity. It is not a calculable, external limitation. Being is not limited by something outside of it that would thus brand it as finite. The finitude of being is an inner, intrinsic finitude. The finitude of being does not mean that being is limited in time and space. Time and space, time-space, utterly belong to being and cannot limit it from the outside. Thus, being is not going to 'run out' and exhaust itself temporally or spatially. The finitude of being does not consist in its limitation in space and time represented as dimensions external to it.

The finitude of being means that being is not absolute. Being needs *Da-sein*, the abyss of time-space. The human being is not automatically equivalent to *Da-sein*—far from it. He is more often 'away' than 'there',[22] which is Heidegger's later characterization of the 'inauthenticity' described at length in *Being and Time*. Man becomes, inhabits, *Da-sein* when he enters into Appropriation, when he belongs to being as Appropriation. This would or will be synonymous with the end of metaphysics as the history of the forgotten-ness of being.

> Metaphysics is the oblivion of Being, and that means the history of the concealment and withdrawal of that which gives Being. The entry of thinking into Appropriation is the equivalent to the end of this withdrawal's history. The oblivion of Being 'supersedes' itself in the awakening into Appropriation. But the concealment which belongs to metaphysics as its limit must belong to Appropriation itself. That means that the withdrawal which characterized metaphysics in the form of the oblivion of Being now shows itself as the dimension of concealment itself. But now this concealment does not conceal itself. Rather, the attention of thinking is concerned with it.
>
> With the entry of thinking into Appropriation, its own way of concealment proper to it also arrives. Appropriation is in itself expropriation. This word contains in a manner commensurate with Appropriation the early Greek *lethe* in the sense of concealing.[23]

The withdrawal of being occurring during the history of metaphysics as the history of the forgottenness of being now could revert to its pristine form of concealment. To once more make use of the distinction between process and structure, the process of withdrawal could turn back into the structure of concealment in the heart of being. Withdrawal, the unmistakable moving away from us of being, could return to us as the sheltering and preserving element in being itself.

But what else does this mean than that presence as such, and together with it the opening granting it, remain unheeded? Only what *aletheia* as opening grants is experienced and thought, not what it is as such. This remains concealed. Does this happen by chance? Does it happen only as a consequence of the carelessness of human thinking? Or does it happen because self-concealing, concealment, *lethe* belongs to *aletheia,* not just as an addition, not as shadow to light, but rather as the heart of *aletheia?* And does not even a keeping and preserving rule in this self-concealing of the opening of the presence from which unconcealment can be granted to begin with, and thus what is present can appear in its presence? If this were so, then the opening would not be the mere opening of presence, but the opening of presence concealing itself, the opening of self-concealing sheltering.

If this were so, then with these questions we would reach the path to the task of thinking at the end of philosophy.[24]

Here we finally have a clear directive. At the end of philosophy—and that means of metaphysics—we come to the path of the task of thinking. The task of thinking now becomes thinking the clearing of presencing concealing itself, the clearing of self-concealing sheltering.

The finitude that Heidegger is attempting to think (in the non-representational sense of *Besinnung* and *Andenken*) here is not only an *inner* finitude; it is an *inward* finitude undetermined by any relation to something outside of it, be that infinity or anything else. The 'limits' constitutive of this finitude secure its intactness and prevent its dispersal into in-finitude or empty nothingness.

But just as being for Heidegger was conceived from the very outset as nonsubstantial, never as objective presence (substance), the finitude of being cannot be thought as limited *substance* either.

When Heidegger speaks of being's need for human being, this does not indicate the finitude of being in the sense that being is lacking something outside itself that it needs in order to complete itself. Human being is not outside of being but utterly belongs to it.

Thus, for Heidegger, we can ultimately say that the finitude of being lies in its being preserved, secure, and inviolate in its own. The hope is that the process of the history of being as metaphysics culminating in the essence of technology might *turn into* the belonging together (identity, Appropriation) of being and human being. This belonging together is not processual, but it is not static either.

The term 'turning' (*die Kehre*) has multiple meanings in Heidegger. The meaning of turning in the following passage is surely a highly significant one: the turning from Framing (the essence of technology) to Appropriation, the belonging together of being and human being.

> *Insight into what is*—this title now names the appropriating event (*Ereignis*) of the turning into being, the turning of the refusal of its presencing into the Appropriating of its true preservation (*Wahrnis*).[25]

EPILOGUE

Imaginary dialogue between Heidegger and a Buddhist, with apologies for possible implausibilities of the personalities.

Buddhist: Professor Heidegger, in the interest of a future dialogue between East and West, I think it admirable that a Western philosopher has finally placed death in the center of the existential situation, unmitigated by hopes for Platonic immortality or Christian promises of an afterlife. I personally am particularly interested in your emphasis on nothingness, a question, of course, not unrelated to the question of death. Today I should very much like to pursue what you say about the question of nothingness and your related conception of the clearing. You yourself have referred to "the inevitable conversation with the East Asian world."[1] Perhaps we might begin by discussing your dialogue between a Japanese and a questioner on the subject of language.[2] I have just reread it, and it is still fresh in my mind. In it, the Japanese referred to emptiness, which for us is the highest name for what you perhaps mean by the word *being*. How do *you* understand the term 'emptiness'?

Heidegger: I believe the Japanese called emptiness *"ku,"* the emptiness of the heaven, what is without limits.

B: Yes.

H: What makes me uneasy is the expression "without limits." When the Greeks spoke of nothingness, they made a sharp distinction between *me on,* relative nothingness, and *ouk on,* absolute nothingness. By absolute nothingness I understand sheer nugatory nothingness, which is indicative of the common aversion to anything not positive and life-affirming. This conception of nothingness is totally blind to the deeply affirmative, creative possibilities of nothingness that are expressed in *me on,* relative nothingness. This nothingness is a *definite,* unique nothingness and belongs to the heart of being.

B: Your objection to absolute nothingness sounds very much like your objection to Rilke's conception of the Open, which you criticized in "What Are Poets For?"

H: Precisely. Not only is Rilke's conception metaphysical, but, beyond that, it is curiously close to the Christian idea of the Infinite. The Open is without all bounds. In the essay you mentioned, I stated that Rilke's Open is precisely what is closed up, uncleared, what draws on in boundlessness, so that nothing can be encountered in it. I myself often used the term 'the Open', but I gradually came to abandon it in favor of the term 'clearing'.

B: What is the difference between the Open and the clearing? This seems to me to be an essential question.

H: You are right. Just think of the image of a clearing in the forest. It is a *defined,* open space in which something can presence and be encountered. In contrast, Rilke's Open is completely indefinite, without all bounds, and nothing can presence or be encountered in it. Rilke's Open is uncleared, opaque, so to speak. It is a boundless, mute, opaque in-finity in which nothing can presence or happen. Presencing must have limits and be defined. The clearing must be structured and attuned (*gefügt und gestimmt*).

B: And yet you yourself consistently say that the Nothing belongs to being. You are one of the first Western thinkers to assert this, and that is partly what draws many Easterners, Buddhists in particular, to your thinking.

H: But by the Nothing I have never meant boundless emptiness.

B: What do you have against the term 'emptiness'? It is an absolutely central word for Buddhists.

H: There can be no presencing in emptiness. Emptiness precludes presencing.

B: It is astonishing to hear you say that. Let us try to discuss this further. Buddhists are now speaking about relative nothingness or emptiness and absolute nothingness or emptiness.

H: That would correspond to the Greek *me on* and *ouk on.* *Ouk on,* absolute nothing, means what I call nugatory nothingness, nothing at all; I reject this concept which coincides with the common understanding of nothing, an "understanding" that exhausts itself in simple aversion. *Me on,* relative nothing, on the other hand, denies something to a thing which belongs to it, and is thus related to it: a kind of keeping at bay, a rejection, a prevention. But the denial, or the not, remains related to the thing, rejecting it and keeping it at bay; thus it is through and through a definite lack, denial, nothingness. It is *this particular* lack.

B: We may mean by relative nothingness pretty much the same thing. Where we differ is in regard to absolute nothingness. Far from regarding absolute nothingness as merely nugatory nothingness or even any kind of *absence* at all, Buddhists experience absolute nothingness or emptiness as the only possibility of experiencing totality, wholeness, fullness.

H: Could you perhaps elucidate that?

B: As you yourself know, the experience of a something or any particular thing precludes the experience of anything else. When I look at a tree—particularly if I objectify it as we all, East and West, tend to do—I see only that tree; I do not see, for example, the flowering bush next to it.

H: But what if I am able to see a tree, for example, the way Van Gogh painted it? Then I would not objectify it, and the experience of the tree would not rigidly exclude other things.

B: Agreed. But there are not many of us who can see a tree the way Van Gogh saw it; the experience is admittedly rare.

H: Rare, but possible.

B: But what if there is a way of seeing the world that opens up and infinitely expands that possibility?—then it would not be rare.

H: That sounds intriguing, but in our period of what I call the history of being, I tend to doubt that it is possible. In the epoch of Framing and technology, it may not be possible to see the world that way. Framing blocks any pristine kind of presencing.

B: I cannot argue with that. What you are speaking of is predominantly an epoch of Western history, and yet it has profoundly affected the East as well. What you call Framing or technology has its roots in the West, but the growth has spread over the entire globe. Nothing can be isolated any longer. Yet you yourself have expressed the hope for an end to Framing and technology, and also to objectifying, calculative thinking.

H: That is true. I have expressed the hope for a more primordial belonging together of man and being, experienced as the Fourfold, the Fourfold of earth and heaven, the godlike ones and the
mortals.

B: But how is the Fourfold to be *experienced?* In your language, where does it presence?

H: The Fourfold presences in the thing, whether that thing
be a jug, a bridge, a tree, or whatever.

B: But how, according to you, can four different 'things' presence in one thing? With this question I am not digressing; I am getting back to a discussion of emptiness. You will see what I mean.

H: I think I already have some idea. Initially, I would answer
that the Fourfold does not consist of 'things' in the ordinary sense,
nor is the thing in which they presence any kind of object, but more
of a possibility, a possible site for the Fourfold to presence. I have
tried to describe how earth, heaven, the godlike ones, and mortals
presence in a jug in my essay "The Thing."

B: Yes, I know that fine essay. We are agreed in what we reject: the separateness of reified objects. What we yet have to try to
clarify is how it is possible for a totality—I take it that the Fourfold
is a kind of totality—to presence in a thing. In that essay, you even
say that what does the vessel's holding, what holds the wine, is the
emptiness of the jug.

H: Yes, but by emptiness I did not mean indefinite emptiness, but rather the *specific* emptiness of *that* jug.

B: Thus, in your terminology, a *me on,* not an *ouk on.* Buddhists feel that in order to attain true affirmation, the negation
must itself be negated. In other words, relative nothingness, *me on,*
must be negated in order to arrive at absolute nothingness or
emptiness.

H: You mean to arrive at some kind of Hegelian synthesis.

B: No. By negating the negation, you arrive at, so to speak,
another dimension of the same reality you started with. There is no
position (thesis) or positing whatever involved. There is no progres-
sion (from thesis to antithesis to synthesis); it is a matter of *pene-
trating* to the very reality of the thing in question, be it a jug, a tree,
or a pebble.

H: You mean the *being* of the thing?

B: I suppose *you* might want to put it that way. But you must remember that Buddhists and also Taoists begin, not with being, but with nonbeing, with nothing. What matters is nothing, not being. But you may not wish to go that far.

H: I would want to somehow get beyond the opposition of being and nothingness.

B: Bravo! There we agree completely. But consider this. If you negate relative nothingness, *me on,* the negation yields the specific thing negated. If you negate non-tree, you wind up with tree again. You end up with the reality of this definite thing. But if you negate absolute nothingness, *ouk on,* the negation of the lack of everything yields everything, absolute reality and fullness.

H: It sounds good, but I would have to have some experience of that.

B: Absolutely. Without the experience of absolute nothingness or emptiness, all you have are meaningless words. You become one of Dōgen's "word-counting scholars."

H: But, at best, absolute nothingness sounds like it might be some kind of *universal.* Absolute nothingness as the universal then subsumes, swallows up, as it were, all the particulars. What I mean by being is absolutely singular and unique.

B: In Buddhism emptiness goes together with *tathata,* suchness. Suchness or all the suchnesses are not subsumed under emptiness, nor are they swallowed up by it. Particular things absolutely remain as they are (as-it-isness, suchness), yet they are paradoxically identical with emptiness.

H: To me, suchness or as-it-isness sounds a bit like Meister Eckhart's *Istigkeit,* isness. If the two are related or indeed are 'the same', then I have an inkling of what you are talking about.

B: The Heart Sutra has the well-known, recurring phrase, "Form is emptiness; emptiness is form." This is a highly paradoxical identity. It is not an identity of mediation of the kind you find in German Idealism, but an immediate identity. Nevertheless, it is not an 'initial' identity; no one starts out with it; this identity has to be *realized;* yet the realization, when it occurs, is immediate.

H: If you have negation, you have mediation.

B: You have perhaps heard the saying, "Before enlightenment mountains are mountains and rivers are rivers. During enlightenment mountains are not mountains and rivers are not rivers. After enlightenment mountains are *really* mountains and rivers are *really* rivers." This does not describe a *process:* you have not gone anywhere. You are *really* where you were in the first place.

H: I believe I can follow that. But why is it not mediation?

B: Because in this case you have not negated anything. All that happens is that a certain habitual, constrained way of seeing drops away; it is shattered. But let us return to the question of negation and emptiness. That, after all, is our main topic.

H: Yes. We must not get off the track.

B: Let us go back to Rilke's Open. You said that in it nothing could presence or be encountered. I assume that by "be encountered" you do not mean a subject encountering an object.

H: No, no. In boundlessness or the Open, things, if we can even speak of things in this case, would simply drift about endlessly. There would be nothing to halt them or bring them to a stand. I cannot encounter something that drifts endlessly. I cannot catch up with it, so to speak. It never achieves a presence. This has nothing to do with subject or object.

B: I follow that. But if the thing were brought to a stand by some kind of limit or barrier, then it would stand opposite, over against me as an ob-ject. As far as I understand the term 'object', an object does not presence; it stands opposite, over against me.

H: I am not talking about an object. For me, the thing is, so to speak, the meeting place for the dimensions of earth, heaven, the godlike ones, and the mortals. There is nothing objective about that.

B: When a Buddhist sees, truly sees, a thing, he does not encounter the thing; he becomes the thing.

H: You would have to explain that.

B: It cannot be explained; it can only be seen. But let us return to your mention of Van Gogh. If we take a Chinese landscape painting, what do we see? Not several or many things as in most Western art—say, a landscape, portrait, or still life—but a vast expanse of emptiness and somewhere, perhaps in a corner, a twig or a leaf.

H: I have seen such paintings. They are very fine.

B: You respond to a painting of emptiness; it is the concept that somehow repels you.

H: I must admit that, for me, boundlessness and any kind of presence or being absolutely preclude each other. What about the twig?

B: The twig could be suchness. The twig, the suchness, lets you see boundless emptiness; boundless emptiness lets you see the twig.

H: So there is a presence within emptiness?

B: Not quite. To go back to the Heart Sutra, "Form *is* emptiness; emptiness *is* form." It is not the case that one sees form *within* emptiness or emptiness *within* form. You yourself have polemicized, in *Being and Time,* against this kind of 'within'.

H: Yes, yes. I am beginning to see what you mean. I guess it is the immediate identity that gives me trouble. Could you say that emptiness is immanent within the form?

B: That is just another within, an 'in which'. Emptiness *is* form.

H: You are right. I think we are beginning to realize that the traditional central concepts of immanence and transcendence are no longer adequate to capture the relation of God and world or, in my language, of being and beings. I myself would no longer state, as I did in *Being in Time,* that being is the absolute *transcendens.* Being is neither transcendent nor is it absolute. All of that belongs to metaphysics and ontotheology.

B: Now we are beginning to get somewhere. Then why does immediate identity cause you so much trouble?

H: Once one has studied Hegel and his critique of Schelling and intuition, it is difficult to be content with immediacy. Above all, Hegel believed in "the hard labor of the concept"—in short, in the transformation of nature or immediacy by Spirit. Immediacy, as it is, is nothing; it only attains significance by being negated and transformed.

B: At least we agree about the necessity of negation.

H: But I don't think we are negating the same thing. Hegel is negating immediacy. You are not.

B: Hegel *believes* he is negating immediacy.

H: Immediacy is what we start out with. What is so mean-ingful about that? Surely meaning enters in with Spirit.

B: Immediacy is precisely *not* what we start out with. For ex-ample, when we first see a tree, we normally think, This is a tree, not a bush. It is a birch tree, not an oak tree. In other words, we classify and categorize the tree. This is not immediate experience.

H: Then what would immediate experience be?

B: First, I have to negate my habitual categorizing and con-ceptualizing. Then I have no tree, no thing, relative no-thingness, not this tree. Finally, I must negate this negation to arrive at ab-solute no-thingness.

H: What is it you then *see?*

B: Suchness.

H: Hegel, of course, could not accept that. What is real for him is the concept, not immediacy. But I think I see what you are getting at.

B: Of course we must not cling to words like *suchness* and *ab-solute nothingness*. They remain fingers pointing at the moon. Words and concepts point to something; as long as we realize that words are not themselves It, they can be helpful. Even, no, *espe-cially* emptiness has to empty itself out. Emptiness itself is empty, nonsubstantial.

H: I completely agree with that. Not with everything you say, but with nonsubstantiality.

B: Now, can we fit nonsubstantiality together with what you mean by Being? Surely for you being is not substance.

H: Not at all! That is why instead of the term 'being', which is heavily burdened with scholastic and ontotheological connota-tions, I have come to prefer more poetic terms such as 'Appropria-tion', 'the Fourfold', and 'Clearing of self-concealing'.

B: The last term, 'Clearing of self-concealing', baffles me. Why concealing?

H: Being does not unconceal itself completely. We do not have clearing alone; we have clearing of self-concealing.

B: I am aware that you say that we *haven't* had pure clear-ing, that being withdraws and abandons us in the course of the his-tory of being, and that now even this abandonment has been forgotten. But does that mean that there *cannot* be pure unconcealment and clearing unmitigated by concealing?

H: Concealing is essential. It is true that in the course of the history of being, concealing has approached distortion, but concealing belongs to being. In fact, you could almost abbreviate and say, "Being is self-concealing." If self-concealing is cleared, then we have an appropriate relation to being.

B: But why is concealing so essential?

H: There is no answer to that, no 'why'. It just is.

B: I beg your pardon. I was not asking for a reason why, a *logos.* I merely fail to understand why concealing is essential. I do understand "clearing." It is a beautiful word. It lets me see transparency, openness.

H: We may have reached an impasse here. I cannot explain. You would have to *see* it.

B: I know just what you are saying. But I cannot *see* concealing. At the end of your lecture "The End of Philosophy and the Task of Thinking," you ask the question whether the name for the task of thinking reads clearing or opening and presence instead of being and time. There it is clearing that names being. Where is concealing?

H: I admit it is absent in that particular formulation. But it still belongs to being. I suppose self-concealing has to do with what I call "the Mystery." Being is never completely unconcealed; it remains Mystery.

B: I like mystery better than self-concealing. I read somewhere that mystery comes from *muein,* to close the mouth. According to that, mystery simply means something that cannot be conceptually expressed; self-concealing, on the other hand, seems to indicate a kind of deliberate willfulness in being, almost a niggardly refusal to unconceal itself.

H: I never intended that with self-concealing. Let us try to get back to seeing, nonobjectifying seeing, or even what you spoke of as absolute nothingness, as the possibility of experiencing totality, wholeness, fullness.

B: Yes. That is perhaps more fruitful for us at this point.

H: I have discussed the experience of nothingness, in *Being and Time,* as the experience of anxiety and, in a lecture course on

Basic Concepts of Metaphysics, as the experience of boredom. Both experiences are completely objectless. In anxiety, things or objects slip away and cease to be of any concern or interest to us. The same thing happens in boredom, but more gradually and imperceptibly with a different feeling-tone from that of anxiety. In fact, I got so fascinated by the phenomenon of boredom that I went on about it for weeks in the lecture course. I heard that one of my colleagues remarked that the discussion of boredom (*Langeweile,* a long while) went on for such a long while that it demonstrated phenomenologically what it was talking about!

B: Why not? We could bore people right out of objectifying, reifying, and substantializing!

H: What I was talking about with both of these phenomena is *mood.* Mood affects and attunes the way in which we see things. It seems to me that Western philosophy has ignored the importance and influence of mood. Its emphasis has all been on rationality and reason. By "mood" I do not just mean feelings and emotions, although they are in some way derivative of mood. Mood comes from mode, way.

B: Way? Oh!

H: These two moods, anxiety and boredom, let us experience the world in a different way. They are absolutely nonobjectifying.

B: That is a step in the right direction. But do they allow us to experience totality?

H: In a way, yes. I have always spoken of beings *as a whole* (*das Seiende im Ganzen*). This "as a whole" overcomes us in the experience of anxiety, boredom, or joy.

B: I do not recall that you ever elaborated upon the experience of joy. An experience of great, indescribable joy usually accompanies the experience of totality. It seems difficult to reconcile joy with anxiety or boredom.

H: What they have in common is the fact that they are objectless.

B: But objectlessness is not sufficient. The experience of release accompanied by great joy is lacking in the experiences of anxiety and boredom.

H: Release? If in anxiety and boredom things are of no concern to you, are you not released from them?

B: Yes, released *from* them. Now, released *whereto?*

H: Well, I suppose to no-thingness.

B: Relative no-thingness or absolute no-thingness?

H: I don't think one can say to relative no-thingness.

B: Thus, released to absolute no-thingness.

H: I'm afraid in this case I'll have to concede that. There is nothing specific or definite about the negation taking place in anxiety and boredom.

B: Now I should like to ask something about the Fourfold.

H: Fine. And since our time is getting short, I also have one more question for you.

B: I shall try to keep my question short. It concerns mirroring, the mirror-play of the Fourfold. I know that one of your major concerns is to step back out of metaphysics. Surely the Fourfold accomplishes this. It is truly not metaphysical.

H: That is true. It is also the reason why it is not readily accessible to everybody, particularly not to the philosophers. A poet would probably understand it immediately.

B: In the essay "The Thing," you stated that mirroring does not portray a likeness. How, then, is mirroring to be thought?

H: Each of the four dimensions of the Fourfold mirrors in its own way the presencing of others. Mirroring thus clears and frees each of the four; none of them insists on its own separate particularity. In this manner the four dimensions of the Fourfold interpenetrate each other. The best way I have found to describe this is to say they mirror each other. It is a dynamic, totally nonsubstantial interrelating.

B: That is extraordinary. You may not realize how close this is to a school of Chinese Buddhism—close to, not identical with.

H: I cannot judge that. Now, it is perhaps time to ask my final question.

B: Yes.

H: I want to know how absolute nothingness can yield *totality*. How is an experience of totality possible and how is it that precisely absolute nothingness should give it to us?

B: Let me first say that if there is self-concealing, it is not possible. Self-concealing and experience of totality are incompatible. You will not be able to agree with that, but it has to be said. As for totality, if it is to be experienced, it has to presence at one time and one place. We cannot experience totality or wholeness cumulatively as a sum by traveling over the entire globe or by living one hundred years.

H: Agreed. Traveling over space and living through time are discursive. When I am in Hong Kong, I am not in Tübingen; when I am eighty years old, I am no longer forty. No discursive experience of totality is possible. Discursiveness precludes totality. Totality can be experienced only simultaneously.

B: Good. The experience of totality or wholeness must be all at once right now and right here. It is not *exclusively* in this right now and right here, but if I am going to experience it, it has to be in *some* right now and here.

H: I understand that. I have just been reading Meister Eckhart who says something like the following (I quote approximately from memory):

> Many masters thought that the soul is only in the heart. That is not so, and great masters have been wrong about this. The soul is wholly, and indivisibly totally in the foot and totally in the eye and in every member. If I take a piece of time, that is neither today nor yesterday. But if I take the *now* (*das Nun*), it embraces *all* time within itself. The now in which God created the world is in this time as near as the now in which I am speaking, and the last judgment is as near to this now as yesterday.[3]

B: That is indeed astonishing! This man experienced totality in the absolute eternal now. I should think that the time encompassed by the creation of the world and the day of last judgment ought to qualify as a totality! I now see that this experience is not absolutely an Eastern prerogative. Professor Heidegger, we have just touched upon a few extremely crucial and highly intriguing topics. For today, let me conclude our conversation with the following quote on boundless openness.

> You shouldn't set up limits in boundless openness, but if you set up limitlessness as boundless openness, you've trapped

yourself. This is why those who understand emptiness have no mental image of emptiness.

If people use words to label and describe the mind, they still don't comprehend the mind.[4]

H: Remarkable insight.

NOTES

Chapter One—The Problem

1. Martin Heidegger, *Being and Time*, trans. Joan Stambaugh (New York: Harper and Row, 1962), p. 499.

2. GA 29/30. *The Basic Concepts of Metaphysics* (Frankfurt am Main: Vittorio Klostermann, 1983), p. 306.

Chapter Two—Concealment as Preservation

1. GA vol. 54, p. 198. Gesamtausgale

2. Ibid., pp. 197–8.

3. Ibid., p. 92.

4. Ibid, p. 95.

5. Ibid, p. 116.

6. *Early Greek Thinking*, p. 114.

7. GA 55, pp. 152–3.

8. *Basic Writings*, p. 196. Cf. also *The End of Philosophy*, trans. Joan Stambaugh (New York: Harper and Row, 1973), p. 43.

9. *Holzwege*, p. 141.

10. Ibid., p. 176.

Chapter Three—Concealing as Strife
with Unconcealing

1. *Holzwege*, pp. 19–20.

2. Ibid., p. 179.

3. Ibid., p. 184.

4. Ibid., p. 25.

5. Ibid., p. 38.

6. Ibid., p. 105.

7. Ibid., p. 185.

8. *Basic Writings,* p. 136.

Chapter Four—Concealing as Distortion

1. GA 54, p. 23.

2. Ibid., p. 41.

3. Ibid., p. 45.

4. Ibid., p. 79.

5. Ibid., p. 135.

6. Ibid., p. 187.

7. Ibid., p. 189.

Chapter Five—Concealment as Process; Nihilism as the History of Being

1. *Nietzsche* IV, trans. Frank A. Capuzzi (New York: Harper and Row, 1982), p. 201.

2. Ibid., p. 208.

3. Ibid., pp. 213–14.

4. Ibid., p. 214.

5. Ibid., p. 217.

6. Ibid., p. 218.

7. Ibid., p. 219.

8. Ibid., p. 220 [minor changes added].

9. Ibid., p. 224.

10. Ibid., p. 225.

11. Ibid., p. 226.

12. *Vier Seminare* (Frankfurt am Main: Vittorio Klostermann, 1977), p. 45.

13. Ibid., p. 104.

14. *Identity and Difference,* trans. Joan Stambaugh (New York: Harper and Row, 1969), p. 29.

15. *Nietzsche IV,* pp. 226–7.

16. *Gelassenheit* (Pfullingen: Günther Neske, 1959), p. 26.

17. Ibid., p. 227.

18. *Nietzsche LV,* p. 232.

19. Ibid., 239.

20. Ibid., 245.

Chapter Six—Framing

1. *Basic Writings,* p. 307.

2. Ibid., p. 309.

3. Ibid., p. 314.

4. *The End of Philosophy,* trans. Joan Stambaugh (New York: Harper and Row, 1973), pp. 66–7.

5. *Vier Seminare* (Frankfurt am Main: Vittorio Klostermann, 1977), pp. 107–8.

Chapter Seven—The Open, the Opening

1. "Hölderlin and the Essence of Poetry" in *Existence and Being* (Chicago: Regnery, 1949).

2. *Parmenides,* p. 226.

3. Ibid., p. 233.

4. Ibid., p. 234.

5. Ibid., p. 237.

6. Ibid., p. 238.

7. *Poetry, Language, Thought,* p. 106.

8. Ibid., pp. 106–7.

9. Ibid., pp. 115–16.

10. Ibid., pp. 119–20.

11. Ibid., p. 120.

12. Ibid., p. 134.

13. Ibid., p. 140.

Chapter Eight—The Open in Heidegger's Conception

1. *Parmenides,* p. 197.

2. Ibid.

3. Ibid., p. 198.

4. Ibid., pp. 199–200.

5. Ibid., p. 201.

6. Ibid., p. 208.

7. Ibid., pp. 212–13.

8. Ibid., pp. 213–14.

9. Ibid., pp. 221–2.

10. Ibid., pp. 223–4.

11. *On Time and Being,* trans. Joan Stambaugh (New York: Harper and Row, 1972), p. 64; translation amended.

12. Ibid., p. 65.

13. Ibid.

14. Ibid., p. 68.

Chapter Nine—Appropriation

1. *Vier Seminare*, p. 108.

2. Ibid., p. 104.

3. *Identity and Difference*, pp. 72–3.

4. *Vier Seminare*, pp. 108–9.

5. Op. cit., p. 29.

6. Ibid., pp. 30–31.

7. Ibid., pp. 36–7.

8. *Poetry, Language, Thought*, pp. 202–3.

Chapter Ten—Return to the Problem

1. *Beiträge*, p. 379.

2. Ibid., p. 308.

3. From the Greek *a*-alpha privativum and *byssos,* ground.

4. Ibid., p. 346.

5. Ibid., pp. 380–81.

6. Ibid., pp. 379–80.

7. Ibid., p. 390.

8. Ibid., p. 391.

9. *Der Satz vom Grund* (Pfullingen: Neske, 1957), p. 93.

10. Ibid., p. 98.

11. *Beiträge*, pp. 387–8.

12. Ibid., pp. 380–87.

13. Cf. Stambaugh, "Nihilism and the End of Philosophy," in *Research in Phenomenology*, vol. XV, 1985.

14. *Nietzsche IV*, p. 214 [with adaptations by the author].

15. Ibid., p. 217.

16. Ibid., p. 220.

17. Ibid.

18. Ibid., p. 226.

19. Ibid., p. 232.

20. Ibid., pp. 239–40.

Chapter Eleven—Schelling's Treatise on Human Freedom

1. *Schelling: On Human Freedom,* trans. James Gutmann (Chicago: Open Court, 1936), p. 93.

2. Ibid., p. 87.

3. Ibid., p. 90.

4. *Nietzsche* IV, p. 244.

Chapter Twelve—Appropriation and Concealment: Concealment as Process and as Structure

1. *On Time and Being,* pp. 22–3.

2. Ibid., p. 41.

3. Ibid.

4. Ibid.

5. Ibid.

6. Ibid., p. 9 [with minor changes]

7. Ibid, p. 23.

8. *Identity and Difference,* p. 71.

9. *Die Fragmente der Vorsokratiker,* Diels and Kranz, (Zürich: Wiedmann, 1971), p. 152. no. 8.

10. *On the Way to Language,* p. 22.

Chapter Thirteen—The Fourfold

1. *Poetry, Language, Thought,* p. 220.

Chapter Fourteen—Nature

1. *Vier Seminare,* p. 89.

2. *Of Human Freedom,* Chicago: Open Court, 1936, quoted in James Gutmann's introduction from Schelling's last work, pp. xlvii–xlviii.

3. *Vorträge und Aufsätze,* Pfullingen: Neske, 1954, p. 126.

4. *Poetry, Language, Thought,* p. 42.

5. Ibid., p. 44.

6. Ibid., p. 49.

7. Ibid., p. 55.

8. Ibid., p. 149.

9. Ibid., p. 178.

10. Ibid., p. 149.

11. *Early Greek Thinking,* trans. Krell and Capuzzi, New York: Harper and Row, 1975, p. 117.

Chapter Fifteen—Mortals and the Godlike Ones

1. *Poetry, Language, Thought,* p. 150.

2. Ibid., p. 178.

3. Ibid., p. 150.

4. Ibid., pp. 178–9.

Chapter Sixteen—The Pure Draft

1. *On The Way to Language,* p. 83.

2. *Poetry, Language, Thought,* p. 105.

3. Ibid., p. 106.

4. *Parmenides,* p. 226.

5. *Poetry, Language, Thought,* p. 120.

6. Ibid., p. 120.

7. Ibid., p. 122.

8. Ibid., p. 127.

9. Ibid., p. 137.

10. Ibid., p. 136.

Chapter Seventeen—The In-finite Relation
(*Verhältnis*)

1. *Erläuterungen zu Hölderlins Dichtung,* Frankfurt am Main: Vittorio Klostermann, 1981, p. 163.

2. Ibid., pp. 170–71.

3. Ibid., p. 166.

4. Ibid., p. 176.

5. Ibid., p. 178.

6. Ibid., p. 61.

7. Ibid., p. 71.

Chapter Eighteen—The Mirror-Play of the Fourfold

1. *Vier Seminare,* p. 104.

2. *Poetry, Language, Thought,* p. 203.

3. Monadology 56, 77 and 83.

4. *Poetry, Language, Thought,* p. 179.

5. Ibid.

6. Ibid.

7. Ibid., p. 181.

8. Ibid., p. 182.

Chapter Nineteen—Beiträge

1. The positioning of this section is due solely to the fact that *Beiträge* first became available for Heidegger's one hundredth birthday, 1989.

2. *Beiträge*, p. 3.

3. Cf. Joseph P. Fell, "Heidegger's Notion of Two Beginnings," in *Review of Metaphysics*, vol. XXV, no. 2. Among the numerous works consulted but not actually cited, the following were especially helpful for the topic of this study: Schürmann: *Heidegger on Being and Acting*, Kockelmans: *The Truth of Being*, Fell: *Heidegger and Sartre*, Dennis Schmidt: *The Ubiquity of the Finite*.

4. *Beiträge*, p. 233.

5. Ibid., p. 91.

6. *Beiträge*, p. 187.

7. Ibid., p. 296.

8. Ibid., p. 297.

9. Ibid., p. 361.

10. Ibid., p. 379.

11. Ibid., p. 380.

12. Ibid., p. 381.

13. Ibid., p. 384.

14. *Der Ab-grund ist Ab*-grund. Ibid., p. 379.

15. Ibid., p. 380.

16. *Beiträge*, p. 380.

17. Ibid., p. 91.

18. Ibid.

19. Ibid., p. 102.

194   *Notes*

20. Ibid., p. 28.

21. Ibid., p. 9.

22. Ibid., p. 6.

23. Ibid., p. 107.

24. *The End of Philosophy*, New York: Harper and Row, 1973, p. 102.

25. *Beiträge*, p. 229.

26. *Beiträge*, p. 235.

27. Ibid., p. 258.

28. Ibid., p. 261.

29. Ibid., pp. 286–7.

30. Ibid., p. 325.

31. Ibid., p. 324.

32. Ibid., p. 342.

33. Ibid., p. 476.

34. Ibid., p. 413.

35. *Identity and Difference*, pp. 64–5.

36. *Identity and Difference*, pp. 407–8.

37. Ibid., p. 255.

38. Ibid., p. 507.

39. Ibid., pp. 196–7.

40. Ibid., p. 323.

41. Ibid., p. 249.

42. Ibid., p. 260.

43. Ibid., p. 237.

44. Ibid., p. 257.

45. *Vier Seminare*, Frankfurt am Main: Vittorio Klostermann, 1977, p. 76.

46. *Beiträge*, p. 282.

47. Ibid., p. 415.

48. *Beiträge,* pp. 507–8.

49. Ibid., p. 411.

50. *Poetry, Language, Thought,* p. 134.

51. *Beiträge,* p. 437.

52. Ibid., pp. 438–9.

53. Ibid., p. 416.

54. *On Time and Being,* p. 9.

55. *Beiträge,* p. 280.

56. Ibid., p. 411.

57. Ibid., p. 241.

58. Ibid., p. 406.

59. *Vier Seminare,* p. 63.

60. Ibid., p. 332.

61. Ibid., p. 350.

62. Ibid., p. 340.

63. *Vier Seminare,* pp. 390–91.

64. *Basic Writings,* p. 196.

65. *Beiträge,* p. 297.

66. Ibid., p. 278.

67. Ibid., pp. 279–80.

68. Ibid., p. 281.

69. Ibid., p. 283.

70. *The End of Philosophy,* p. 41.

Chapter Twenty—Conclusion

1. *Poetry, Language, Thought,* p. 200.

2. *Identity and Difference,* p. 68.

3. This was precisely Heidegger's own reservation about my initial translation of *Ereignis* as "event of appropriation." Cf. also *Vier Seminare,* p. 103. "The first reference makes it clear that the French word *avenement* (event) is totally inappropriate to translate *Ereignis.* We then again adopt the translation attempted for "Time and Being;" *Ereignis: appropriement.*"

4. *Identity and Difference,* pp. 36–7.

5. *On Time and Being,* pp. 52–3.

6. *Vier Seminare,* p. 104.

7. Ibid., p. 105.

8. Ibid., p. 102.

9. Ibid., p. 103.

10. *On Time and Being,* p. 17.

11. *Vier Seminare,* p. 122.

12. *On Time and Being,* p. 22.

13. Ibid., pp. 22–3.

14. *Poetry, Language, Thought,* pp. 178–9 [with minor changes]

15. Ibid., p. 179.

16. *On Time and Being,* p. 65.

17. *Beiträge,* p. 428.

18. *On Time and Being,* p. 54.

19. *Vier Seminare,* pp. 108–9.

20. *Beiträge,* pp. 268–9.

21. Ibid., p. 488.

22. Cf. *Beiträge,* pp. 301–2, 323–5.

23. *On Time and Being,* p. 41.

24. Ibid., p. 71.

25. *Die Technik und die Kehre,* Pfullingen: Neske, 1962, p. 44.

Epilogue Notes

1. *The Question Concerning Technology,* trans. William Lovitt, New York: Harper and Row, 1977, p. 158.

2. In *On the Way to Language.*

3. *Deutsche Predigten und Traktate,* München: Hanser Verlag, 1955, p. 195.

4. *Zen Essence,* trans. Thomas Cleary, Boston: Shambala, 1989, p. 50.

INDEX

Anaximenes, 88
andenken, 18, 30
animals, 2, 36–39, 95, 97, 124, 153, 161
Anselm, 141
apocalyptic, 14
Appropriation, 26, 33–34, 50, 53–59, 62–68, 73, 75–81, 106, 111–112, 114, 117, 119, 122–123, 128–129, 142, 145–146, 148, 153–158, 160–167, 169, 178
Aristotle, 22, 60, 81, 113–115, 133, 136, 153, 159
Augustine, 136
Austrag, perdurance, 75, 77, 81, 106, 118, 132, 135, 153–155, 163

Baader, 71–72
Blake, 105
Böhme, 71–72, 85–86
Búddhism, 119

Cartesian, 164
Cusanus, 138

dialectic, 16, 100–102
Dōgen, 175
draft, 93–98
duality, 2

Eckhart, 91, 140, 143, 175, 182
eschatology, 122, 135
eternity, 1, 12, 134
Expropriation, 75, 78–79, 107–108, 153, 155

Fink, 2
Fourfold, 50–51, 64–67, 79, 82, 92, 99, 103, 105, 108, 111, 123, 129–

130, 141, 145, 148, 153, 161–165, 174, 178, 181
Framing, 28–29, 31–34, 50, 53–59, 113–114, 123, 126, 130, 153, 161–165, 174, 178, 181
freedom, 46

Gadamer, 85, 123
Gelassenheit, 31
God, the gods, the last god, 1, 64, 71, 83, 85, 91–92, 102, 112, 124, 132, 139–142, 149, 161, 166, 177

Hegel, 2, 55, 77, 99–100, 137, 141, 143, 165, 174, 177–178
Heraclitus, 5, 13, 67, 79, 88, 96, 106, 118
Hofstadter, 93
Hölderlin, 29, 36, 80, 91–92, 98–100, 146

idea, eidos, 14

Kant, 2, 11, 47, 53, 55, 61, 117, 147, 159, 164
Kierkegaard, 19, 115–116, 118, 122

Leibniz, 39, 47–48, 64, 107, 150
Lichtung, 2, 33, 35, 49, 62, 67, 94, 163

mirror-play, mirroring, 103–108, 162–163, 181

Nagarjuna, 67
Newton, 61, 81, 142
nihilism, 21–29, 66, 68–70, 74, 120, 126